BORN
FOR
THIS

**HOW TO FIND THE WORK
YOU WERE MEANT TO DO**

Chris Guillebeau

D0066862

PAN BOOKS

First published 2016 by Crown Business, an imprint of the
Crown Publishing Group

First published in the UK 2016 by Macmillan

This paperback edition published 2018 by Pan Books
an imprint of Pan Macmillan
20 New Wharf Road, London N1 9RR
Associated companies throughout the world
www.panmacmillan.com

ISBN 978-1-4472-9751-2

1 3 5 7 9 8 6 4 2

A CIP catalogue record for this book is available from the British Library.

Illustrations by Doug Neill/www.dougneill.com
Illustration on p. 280 by Fred Haynes

Printed and bound by CPI Group (UK) Ltd, Croydon, CR0 4YY

For Kenneth L. B. Dauer,

my brother and friend

Contents

Plan of Attack

A headline from the *Onion* proclaimed, "Man Convinces Himself He Has the Job of His Dreams." The job, as you might expect from a satirical newspaper, is a soul-crushing and tedious one. Yet because the man sees no alternative, he decides he really likes it. "It's wonderful that I'm trapped here for the foreseeable future," he says.

The best satires relate to real life in some way. Many people really *are* stuck in soul-crushing jobs, with no escape route in sight. If you find yourself trapped for the foreseeable future, you have two obvious options: settle or make a trade-off.

In the first scenario, you accept that there's no way out, and you continue working the soul-crushing job that steals your joy. You spend a third of your life doing something you don't like, but you decide not to take any steps to change that situation. This first scenario is not actually that unusual—plenty of people do this. They can't see any alternatives, so they disengage from work and try to find meaning and purpose elsewhere.

In the second scenario, you decide to live frugally, working a job that supports your basic needs without taking up all your time. You don't love your work, but that's okay, because you love other things. Or maybe the kind of work you love doesn't pay all that well, so you accept the sacrifice for what you receive in return.

There's nothing fundamentally wrong with either choice, but neither is that exciting. What if you *don't* want to settle? What if you want to find the kind of work that you truly love and you *don't* want to eat ramen noodles every night? Why can't you have it all?

Happily, you can. As you'll see throughout this book, some people manage to find this work. They've won the career lottery, and the results weren't all determined by chance. Whether through their own brilliance or, more likely, as a result of trial and error, they've found the work they were born to do—and that's what makes all the difference.

This book will help you find that thing, too. If you don't want to choose between the two undesirable options, this book will show you a third way.

The book consists of two major sections. In the first section, you'll master a series of lessons that will help you understand what you want and how to get it. In the second section, you'll explore a menu of options designed to help you implement those lessons through a variety of strategies and tactics.

Everything you'll learn in both sections is highly practical. Not everything will apply to you, but that's okay—it's a big book. Choose what excites you, and focus on what will bring you closer to your goals.

This book will also challenge many popular beliefs about the way we live and work. As you'll see, some of these conventional assumptions about what a dream career should look like are misguided or simply wrong. Fortunately, there's a better way, a way that will lead you to the work you were born to do. This book will help you find it.

TERMS OF ENGAGEMENT

Because we're changing the world together, the book includes a few different words and phrases that you may not have encountered before. Here's a quick guide to some of them:

- *Escapology:* the art of leaving a job or situation that doesn't meet your needs
- *Serially resetting:* the concept of changing your life and work every few years
- *Flow:* the all-encompassing feeling you get from working well at something you enjoy

- *Side hustle:* a means of earning money apart from your job

- *Digital asset:* an income-earning project that exists entirely online

- *Gold rush:* a short-term opportunity to make a lot of cash

- *Umbrella profession:* a career consisting of multiple jobs or roles, but all under a unifying theme

My hope is that by the time we're done together, these concepts—and the many others you'll learn throughout the book—will provide you not just a whole new vocabulary but also an entirely new way of thinking about how you live and work.

MISSION OBJECTIVES

This isn't a book that tells you how to quit your job and work for yourself (I already wrote one of those). There's no one-size-fits-all model for a dream career, and not everyone wants to work entirely on their own.

Even if you receive a regular paycheck and have no intention of ever starting a business, it's important to understand that you are still essentially self-employed. No one will look out for your interests as much as you will, so you should make active decisions and take responsibility for your own success as much as possible. This book will give you an edge in both of those areas. Even if you have absolutely no desire to start your own business and are perfectly happy working for a conventional employer, there are plenty of tactics and strategies for turning that job into the work you were born to do.

Lastly, please note that this book is action-oriented. You'll learn why it's important to do certain things, but you can also put a number of tools to use right away. If you're in a hurry, I've listed some bookmarks to instant action plans for you below. For best results, however, don't skip over the Joy-Money-Flow model beginning on page 37. We'll be referring to it throughout the rest of the book.

- Make more money: pages 169–171

- Master the job hunt: pages 211–213

- Solve career dilemmas: pages 126–128

- Hack your existing job: pages 226–232

- Quit your job on good terms: page 73

- Negotiate a better salary or benefits: pages 234–237

- Turn a side hustle into a full-time gig: pages 176–178

- Be the best boss you ever had: pages 77–81

- Build a career around your many skills, passions, and interests: pages 281–283

There are many more strategies and action plans like these throughout the next 13 chapters. In different ways, the goal of each is to help you make huge changes and major improvements in your career.

If you've read this far, I'm guessing that you don't want to settle, and you don't want to suffer. Let's work together to find something *much* better.

"For a long time I thought I should find some passion. Now I realize that passion is not uncovered, it is created. But most people never put in the effort required to get good at something to the point where you grow to love it. I think the passion myth is the number one reason my friends are miserable at their jobs."

—MELODIE, AGE 25,
SYSTEMS AND PROCESSES ARCHITECT

1

Flip the Script

OBJECTIVE:

Choose the Winning Ticket to Your Career Lottery

There's more than one possible path to career success, but you want to find the best one—the thing you were born to do. You want to win the career lottery and discover a job or vocation that doesn't feel like work. Achieving this goal will require changes in mindset, strategy, and action.

If you won the lottery tomorrow, how would your life be different?

Some people might dash straight out to the luxury car

lot, and then drive home in a shiny new toy before booking a Caribbean vacation.

Others might pay off their debt and invest the rest for a comfortable future.

Still others might shrug and give the money to charity.

When it comes to their jobs and careers, different members of our group of hypothetical lottery winners would probably choose different responses. Some people would quit immediately, walking out with no notice. Others would use the experience to reflect on what they *really* wanted to do, and then proceed with the security of having all the money they needed to take the risks to pursue the thing they always dreamed of—whether it's opening a surf shop in Bora Bora, founding a nonprofit in sub-Saharan Africa, or building a tech startup.

Some people, perhaps the truly lucky ones, would look at their lottery winnings and say, "You know, this money's great, but I like what I'm doing enough to stay. Maybe I'll take that vacation on the beach, and maybe I'll buy that car I've always wanted, but then I'll drive it back to my office after a week of sunbathing."

In case you're wondering, none of these answers is the single "right" one. When you win the lottery, it's your money to do with as you please. And even if you love your job, winning the lottery would probably encourage you to reevaluate. Do you love your job so much that you'd do it if you didn't need the money?

Work isn't everything in life, but we spend a great deal of our lives at work. Some people, it seems, really do have it all. These people take to their working roles as if it's the absolute best possible fit for them—it's as though they were born to fulfill a certain role. If you've ever worked on something you took great pleasure in, yet you also got paid for it, you know what this is about. And if you haven't experienced this career bliss yourself, you may have observed it in others.

Ever come across a childhood friend whom you'd lost track of for many years? Maybe he pops up on a social network, or maybe you run into her at the coffee shop. Wherever it is, you hear what that person has been doing for the past 10 or 20 or more years, and you realize it makes perfect sense. *Of course* she became a lawyer—she was always detail-oriented and inquisitive. *Of course* he went into teaching—he was always patient and methodical.

These are the winners of the career lottery; they are people who found what they were meant to do. They're happier because of it, and they are likely more successful, too.

Whatever it was, those people have essentially picked up a winning lottery ticket to the world of work. That's the goal for all of us: to find work that feels like play, yet also has meaning *and* a good paycheck attached to it.

Winning a gazillion dollars in the lottery would be nice, but finding what you were meant to do is far more important. This book will help you win a different kind of lottery—not the kind where someone descends on your doorstep with a oversized check, ready to send you straight to that car dealership or Prada store.

It's better.

"WHAT DO YOU DO FOR A LIVING?"

It's the question you've probably heard a thousand times, whether at parties, networking events, your kid's soccer game, or any other number of places. Depending on what's happening in your life at the moment, the question may fill you with excitement, dread, or something in between.

The question, of course, is "What do you do?" In these situations, it usually means "What do you do for work?" As I was writing this book, I asked this question of hundreds of people. Here are a few of their answers, presented in abbreviated form.

The acupuncturist: "I help people who have health problems that conventional medicine has been unable to explain or treat, and those who are looking for a more natural approach to health and well-being."

The online community manager: "I play a game of whack-a-mole all day. In real-life terms, I'm a community manager. I do everything from business owner seminars to media liaising, party planning to event sponsorships, speaking socially on community marketing to late-night troll fights."

The potter: "I tell people I'm retired. After working for 'the man' for so many years, I *do* feel like I'm retired. Don't be fooled—I actually work harder now than ever, but I love what I do, so only about 20 percent feels like work, and that is the marketing and bookkeeping."

The nomad: "I don't have a standard answer yet. Sometimes I say I'm a writer. Other times I say I'm a filmmaker.

If I'm feeling particularly bold, I might say I live in an RV and travel, and leave it at that."

The answers to "What do you do?" can be so much more diverse and interesting than most people realize, especially when these answers are more than just vague descriptions like "I'm a teacher" or "I work for a magazine." Even more interesting than the answers to "What do you do?," however, is the rarely-asked follow-up of what *led* them to their answer. After all, with all the countless career paths and options out there, how *do* people find that one thing they were born to do?

"HOW DID YOU GET THERE?"

There may be a few superhumans out there who know from age five exactly what they want to do when they grow up, and what form it will take. For the rest of us, it's almost never that simple. Jobs and careers don't fall from the sky to land at our feet, where we simply pick them up and accept them as the perfect fit for life.

Simply put, the process of discovery unfolds a bit differently for most people. As we advance throughout a career (or series of careers), most of us have a number of different work experiences ranging from frustrating to awesome. You can learn something from any job, of course, but most of the time we learn as much about what we *don't* want as what we do.

When I asked hundreds of people who found the work they were "born to do" what paths they took to become the acupuncturist, the civil servant, the teacher, or whatever their current profession is, one theme ran through all their responses: the search took time and effort, and the path had lots of twists and turns, but they all kept working toward it. They believed in the goal, and when they encountered obstacles, they found ways around them.

You may be familiar with "The Road Not Taken," the classic poem by Robert Frost. The poem is about arriving at a path that diverges and having to choose a single direction. In the end, the poet chooses "the road less traveled," and we're told that it "made all the difference." Great poem! But guess what? Maybe the choice of road didn't matter after all. Because in real life, there are many possible paths that can lead us to that lottery-winning job or career.

What if there was a sequel to "The Road Not Taken," written from the perspective of going back in time and making the opposite choice? It probably wouldn't be as poetic: "Hey, everyone, I went back to that road I ignored before. Turns out I got to where I wanted to go anyway! Either choice would have been okay."

The Pulitzer Prize belongs to Frost, not me—but the point is that when it comes to the life choices we make, there really is more than one path.

Not only is it true that there's more than one path you can pursue in life, it's also true that you can be happy any number of ways. Even so, some paths are better than others. Sure, you could be happy in a variety of situations—

but couldn't you be *happier* doing some things as opposed to others?

And if it's true that some paths are better than others, then there's probably one path that's best of all. There's a perfect fit somewhere, one that leads to a feeling of total fulfillment and satisfaction that only comes from waking up every day and getting paid to do something you love.

That's why our goal here isn't just happiness: it's to find the thing *you* were born to do.

JOINING THE CIRCUS

Let's say your dream is to run away and join the circus. Maybe you've always been enchanted by clowns ("How *do* they all get in that tiny car?"), or perhaps you've been practicing your tightrope act in the backyard when you should have been doing your homework. Great. So what are your next steps?

Your quest will probably begin with some sort of research.

You may visit a traveling circus and ask to speak to who-ever's in charge of hiring. You may go online and search for circus jobs. Somehow you'll uncover more information on qualifications (must be good with animals), working conditions (never a dull moment), salary (enough to live on, but not much more), benefits (free peanuts), and the hiring process.

Soon you score an interview for the role of elephant trainer, and ultimately land the job. Congratulations! You report to the elephant tent to begun your inaugural as-signment, full of joy and hope. After a few weeks on the job, however, you realize that joining the circus isn't all it's cracked up to be. The running away part was fun; the cleaning up after the elephants, not so much. You learned what you liked and what you didn't.

So you move on and change roles, getting a job in the ticket sales department. At first you appreciate the new set of responsibilities and the freedom from cleaning up after elephants. But you soon discover that work in the ticket office not only is boring but also requires you to report to duty several nights a week and every weekend. You then decide to leave the circus altogether and do what your par-ents suggested in the first place: you get a cushy office job in ad sales.

But—and this probably doesn't come as a surprise—working for a big corporate company isn't the right fit for you, either. You spend the weeks counting down to Friday night, until one day you're in a meeting with a client who runs a boutique clothing line. A lightbulb goes off in your head. Finally, you realize that designing circus-themed T-shirts was the work you were "born to do" all along.

This is a highly simplified example, but the point is that when you're starting out in the world of work, you probably don't know exactly what you want, at least not right away—and that's normal. Figuring it out takes time and experience, and probably some setbacks along the way. Finding the work you were meant to do is rarely a linear journey. It's a process of exploring many little twists and turns that lead us to the place we ultimately belong.

THE WINNING TICKET

Let's go back to our group of lottery winners. How did they get so lucky? Does it all come down to chance, or did they make smart decisions along the way that led to the appearance of luck?

The first thing to notice is that even in a retirement plan as unreliable as the lottery, you still need to enter to win. Without a ticket, you have zero chance of success.

Also, lottery winners didn't just purchase the ticket—they also had to follow up with at least a few actions. If they bought the winning ticket and never checked the numbers, the choice to buy the ticket was meaningless.

Finally, they had to present themselves as winners, sign all the disclosure forms, agree to pay all required taxes, and have their photo taken while holding up that ridiculously oversized check.

These actions may seem simple, but every year millions of dollars in winnings (real money!) are never claimed. Even lottery winners determined completely by luck have to make all-or-nothing choices to ensure they collect their winnings.

Now for some great news: while the actual lottery is nearly impossible to win, *the career lottery isn't*. This is very important! If the actual lottery is set up properly, there's no way to hack it. You win or you lose—and most of us lose, of course—according to the laws of probability and other variables that are completely outside your control.

With the career lottery, however, you have a great deal of influence over the results. The actions you take now will directly affect the opportunities available to you in the future. That's why it's so important to take the right kinds of actions. If you plan strategically, you can greatly increase your odds of tremendous success.

In short, we want to be lucky—at least as much as we can control our luck—but we also want to make the right decisions along the way.

The Path to Lottery Winnings

Decisions: make the right ones
Luck: increase it wherever possible

OUR GOAL: FLIP THE SCRIPT

Consciously or not, many people tend to choose paths in life by following a preexisting script. By "script" I mean any expectation or assumption about how we should act. Whether in the workplace or greater society, some scripts and norms are important for social cohesion. For example, regardless of our politics, most of us pay taxes because we understand that public goods cost money, and because we don't want to go to jail. This is a good script to follow, generally speaking.

Many other scripts and norms, however, exist merely out of tradition, regardless of whether they're still relevant, or to preserve an existing power structure. Even worse, some exist for no discernible reason whatsoever. And when it comes to careers, social scripts can be particularly unhelpful. You may be discouraged from the kind of thinking or actions you need to find your dream job or career. For example:

- *Script #1:* Entry-level positions should lead to junior management positions, which should eventually become higher management positions (sometimes regardless of the skills of the employees in question), with the goal being to work your way up to the "C-suite," or the corner office.

- *Script #2:* Everyone has a specific "career niche" that they should pigeon-hole themselves into— and once you find yours, don't bother trying to expand or break free of it by exploring other opportunities, skills, or roles.

- *Script #3:* If a career opportunity—any opportunity— comes your way, take it. You'll probably get this chance only once, so don't blow it.

- *Script #4:* Everyone should work 35 to 40 hours a week, mostly in the office, usually on the same days and times (even though research shows that this is largely an unproductive schedule for most people).

Scripts like these, and others that limit the range of paths you can follow or outcomes you can achieve, are at best misguided. Other times they are simply wrong.

Throughout the book, I'll show you how you can get much better results by "flipping the script" and taking an approach that's the opposite of what you may have heard before. When you flip the script, you either update, remix, or in some cases turn the traditional career advice on its head. Consider these alternative ideas:

• *Revised script #1: Don't think like a CEO.*

Blogs and magazines are full of advice columns on "how to invest like Warren Buffett" or "how to manage like Steve Jobs." If you have a billion dollars sitting around, Warren's a great guy to mentor you. For everyone else, Warren would be the first to say that you'll probably achieve better returns by investing in index funds and letting your money grow on its own. Similarly, by most accounts, Steve Jobs was a brilliant designer—and a harsh manager who valued products over people and sometimes left employees cowering in his wake. Is that who you really want as your role model?

Since most of us aren't Warren or Steve, we can't simply apply the same tactics and expect similar results. We need to think for ourselves and find our own tactics. A better plan is to emulate the guy in the slightly smaller office who loves his job, gets along with everyone, and actually has a life outside work.

• Revised script #2: Don't "find a niche"; live a well-rounded life.

Somewhere along the way, you may have been given some terrible advice to choose a niche. But in the vast majority of jobs, specialization is hugely overrated. Some people do find a niche, and they focus on that specialization to the exclusion of all others. Many others, though, excel in environments that reward a more complex blend of skills, talents, and interests. If you've ever been presented with a choice between two undesirable outcomes and you said, "I'd like door number three," you already know there's another way.

Again, the goal is to find what's best for you, not choose from someone else's list of cookie-cutter choices.

• Revised script #3: If you miss one opportunity, there will be others.

Most of us have a deep-seated fear of making the wrong career choice. We tend to stick with what we know, especially when it's "good enough." Yet most career choices can be changed or even reversed. Changing it up is not only normal but also often better. Richard Branson put it best: "Business opportunities are like buses. There's always another one coming."

It's not just business opportunities that are like buses; opportunities of all kinds are always zooming by. If you miss out on one, you can usually hop on another.

• Revised script #4: There's more than one way to work.

Think about the people you know who are blissfully happy in their jobs. Maybe they have a great job with one of those companies that offers unlimited vacation and the opportunity to set your own hours. Maybe they're able to work from home. Or maybe they prefer to work with a team—but they have a great team. If you had the choice of two jobs with equal pay but one offered better working conditions and more flexibility, wouldn't you choose that one?

READING THIS BOOK WILL HELP YOU "LEVEL UP"

I'll promise you one more thing before you read any further: this book is not about marginal improvement. If your job sucks, gaining the right to take off early one Friday a month won't make much of a difference. If you're $80,000 in debt, a 4 percent raise won't pay off your creditors. You don't need to make small changes; you need to *level up*.

This book is designed to help you do just that. I've spent the past 10 years traveling the world and studying different kinds of careers. When talking with people who describe their dream job, I've noticed that they tend to use very similar language. Comments like these are common:

> *I feel like I've won the career lottery.*
>
> *I can't believe I get paid for this. Don't tell anyone, but I like it so much I'd do it for free.*
>
> *Work doesn't feel like work. It often feels like play, and even when it's hard, it's usually meaningful.*

Sounds nice, doesn't it? That's how it feels when you find your dream job or otherwise create the perfect circumstances for how you'll spend a third of your waking hours.

It's time to pick out *your* winning lottery ticket. Where will it take you?

"A dream job looks different for everyone. For some it's passive income. For some it's corporate. For some it's working 1:1 with clients. For some it's being able to work from anywhere. In the end, it's what freedom feels and looks like to each one of us."

—CAROLINE, AGE 34, NATUROPATH

2

Your Money and Your Life

OBJECTIVE:

Have Both

You don't have to choose between doing what you love and making a good living. In this chapter, you'll learn to use the Joy-Money-Flow model to understand your preferred work style and get clearer about your goals.

When you're an adult, you get the "What do you do?" question a lot. But when you were a kid, you probably heard a very different variation of that question at least once: "What do you want to be when you grow up?"

Many of us heard it more than once, from teachers, parents, and other authority figures who encouraged us to dream big and answer with something specific. And indeed, kids often answer this question with wildly ambitious answers like president, astronaut, or professional athlete. Of course, as adults we know that these are unrealistic and out-of-reach careers for most people, but to a child dreaming of his or her future, there's no limit to the imagination.

Do you remember how you answered this question?

Maybe you dreamed of doing something your parents did. If your mom was a doctor, perhaps that sounded good. You liked the idea of helping people, and the hospital seemed like an interesting place to work. Or maybe your dad was an architect and you went to his office one day and saw some cool drawings of big buildings. Maybe that caught your interest and you decided "architect" was as good an answer as any.

Or maybe your aspirations weren't so high-minded, and Mom and Dad weren't your career role models. Did you want to be the mail carrier who drove the fun little car? The supermarket check-out guy who always seemed so happy to see you? The person in charge of that awesome Zamboni machine at a hockey game? It makes sense if you did, because what we see is what we emulate.

In my case, I had a combination of two career dreams, both of which came from my dad. He worked as an aerospace engineer, supporting shuttle launches in the early 1980s and then writing code for Boeing, before he retired to write novels. One early memory stands out. He took me to his office during some sort of test for the space shuttle and gave me an assignment. I don't remember all the details, and I certainly didn't understand them at the time, but I had the impression that it was something important. My assignment was to watch a specific measurement gauge and tell my dad if the needle went above a certain number.

It's probably fair to assume that the safety of the astronauts or the future of NASA did not depend on my close attention to the measurement under my watch. At the age of six, though, that's exactly what I thought was happening. The entire space industry was counting on me! When the test was pronounced a success, I took pride in my contribution—and then I was ready for lunch.

I don't recall where my dad took me to eat after that critical assignment at NASA, but I have a good guess. More often than not, we went to Burger King. I *loved* that place. If I could have eaten at Burger King every day, I'd have been a very happy six-year-old. True, I sometimes had to make tough choices: fries or onion rings? vanilla shake or apple pie? But aside from these dilemmas, I was content with my double cheeseburger and packets of ketchup.

And that's why, at the age of six, whenever an adult asked me, "What do you want to be when you grow up?," my answer was a toss-up. Sometimes I wanted to work with the astronauts, and other times I wanted to work at Burger King. Both careers seemed equally exciting and fulfilling. Of course, I had yet to truly understand what was involved with either one.

GROWING UP AND MAKING DECISIONS

Being asked what you hope to grow into is normal when you are a kid. Sooner or later, though, you reach a certain age where people stop asking—or if they do ask, the tone of the question becomes ominous. Suddenly "What are your dreams? You can do anything you want" becomes "What are you going to do with your life? You'd better figure it out soon."

To many adults, a child whose greatest aspiration is to work at a fast-food restaurant is amusing. But an adult who harbors no greater ambition than deep-frying processed potatoes isn't normally granted much respect.

By the same token, a six-year-old who says he wants to be an astronaut is regarded as adorable, whereas an adult— aside perhaps from a few MIT graduates—who voices the same ambition is thought to be deluded. Once you pass the daydreaming stage of adolescence, realities and practicalities settle in, and you have to make real decisions. You have to decide about education, specialization, internships, or first jobs, and so on. Suddenly the choices seem overwhelmingly limitless. You may join the military, which conveniently pays for education in exchange for an extended commitment of service. You may want to be a doctor, lawyer, or engineer. You may want to pursue a career in the arts or in finance, or work in the media. You may want to do something totally different.

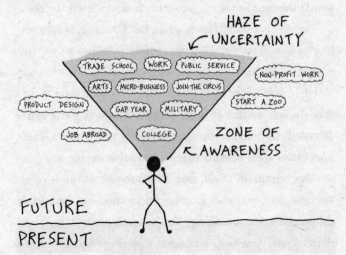

No matter your choice, you'll probably jump into it with limited information and without a full understanding either of how to get there or of what the landscape will look like when you finally arrive. And to complicate matters further, throughout the next few years all sorts of things may happen to change the course of those initial decisions. After an initial investigation into something you thought you'd enjoy, perhaps a college class or an internship or a first job, you might discover that it's not your thing after all.

Once I abandoned my dreams of working at NASA or Burger King, I thought I'd be good at accounting, so I chose it as a major during my first year of college. My professors thought differently, and they encouraged a rapid change by returning my early exams with dismal marks. Sure, I probably could have persevered, studied extra hard, and proved them wrong—but my heart wasn't in it. Accounting clearly wasn't the best fit for me, so I switched to something else.

I made this switch fairly early, but for some, reality sets in a bit later. You may get a degree in something only to discover that the field you were interested in has become outdated, or you might start looking for a position only to find that the job market in your proposed field is particularly crowded. Or maybe you start a family, and those choices affect the career options that are available to you.

Most common of all, and no matter what course of action you take, you may stumble into something completely different as you go along. You may discover a skill you didn't know you had, a passion you never thought you'd have the chance to pursue, or a new job opportunity you never expected. Maybe a former colleague calls to offer you a job at his new company, or a part-time business partnership with a friend from college turns into a *real business*. You didn't plan for it, but all of a sudden you're doing something you never before considered.

The point is that careers are rarely as ordered or intentional as we tend to assume. When we're just beginning adulthood, most of us don't *really* know what we want to do for the next 40 to 60 years of our working life. We have ideas and dreams, but the future is murky. Much remains to be unlocked. Many things may change along the path to finding the work you were born to do.

THE SIMPLE FORMULA FOR THE WORK YOU WERE BORN TO DO: JOY-MONEY-FLOW

Another tenet of traditional career advice is that everyone is different and we all want different things. It's true that every individual has a unique set of skills and interests, and that our backgrounds and contexts are naturally different. But do we all truly want different things? Maybe it's not so complicated: for the most part, we all want to find a career that meets the same few specific needs.

Despite our differences, most of us want a balanced life full of work that brings happiness and prosperity. As much as possible, we want to do something we enjoy. We want to put our skills to good use. And ideally, we don't want to face a false choice between love or money—we'd like to do what we love *and* be well compensated for it.

Put simply, here's what we're looking for:

- Something that makes us happy (joy)
- Something that's financially viable (money)
- Something that maximizes our unique skills (flow)

Remember the goal of this book: to help you win the career lottery and find the work you were meant to do. There's more than one path to this ideal world, but without *all* of these characteristics being met, you won't have a perfect match. It's entirely possible to do something you love that doesn't pay well. It's also possible to get paid well for something you dislike, or something you just tolerate—plenty of people essentially forge a compromise, putting up with a bad situation in exchange for a good paycheck. Finally, it's also possible to enjoy what you do or get paid well for it (or both), but to still lack that sense of all-encompassing flow, where the hours pass like minutes because you're so completely in the zone of doing something you're really good at.

None of those situations is what you want, though. To find the work *you* were born to do, you need the right combination of joy, money, *and* flow.

Here's the rest of the story of how I found mine.

MAKING A LIVING, FROM BURGER KING TO BASKETBALL

A lot of career advice begins right back at age six. It certainly did for me, back when I was busy conducting critical tests for NASA and convincing my dad to take me to Burger King as often as I could. "You can do anything you want," adults usually promise, without any explanation or assurance of how "anything" is possible. Nice as it might sound to our young ears, this advice is absurd. There are definitely some things you aren't going to do, and there's no shortage of things you *shouldn't* do. But that's okay—in fact, it's good.

By the time I was 12 years old, I no longer wanted to work at Burger King. Now I had a new ambition: to play professional basketball. I practiced hundreds of free throws in my backyard, faithfully reenacting the scene in which I scored the final basket in the NBA championship. *You're welcome, everyone. I'm ready to be doused with Gatorade!*

Never mind that I'd never played on a team or even in a real game. Clearly, this was one fantasy that wasn't going anywhere. There's probably a story floating around about someone who became a professional basketball player through sheer determination and hard work, but the reality is, no matter how hard I practiced, I wouldn't ever make the NBA. I don't want to crush your own childhood dreams, but whether it's becoming the president of the United States or being a test pilot for jetpacks, there are certain futures that just aren't going to happen, either for lack of skills, lack of aptitude, lack of opportunity, or some combination of the above. The reality is that there are some career fantasies you'll never achieve no matter how hard you try . . . so whatever those are for you, they shouldn't be your goals.

A few years after my childhood service to NASA and the backyard fantasies of taking my NBA team to the championship ran their course, I had to start making some real choices. I went to college and began shopping around the course catalog. That initial foray into studying accounting was quickly discarded when I struggled to make passing grades. As I took other classes, I discovered that I enjoyed the field of sociology. I loved learning about how people define themselves in relation to others, and how different groups interact and evolve over time. Last but not least, I certainly displayed more of an aptitude for the subject than I had for accounting.

I earned my degree in sociology and proceeded to a short-lived graduate program, but by the time I was there my interests had further evolved. I enjoyed the topics I was studying, but the opportunities in those fields were limited without several more years of education. My night job, loading boxes on a truck for FedEx, held little enjoyment or advancement potential, so it was also highly unlikely to turn into the career of my dreams.

Meanwhile, I had begun to moonlight—literally, since much of the process took place after I got off work at FedEx at 2:00 a.m. and before I had to be in class at 10:00 a.m.—by buying and selling things online. Though I never managed to excel in those accounting classes, it turned out I was actually pretty good at making money and operating a small business.

You may have noticed that I haven't used the *m*-word—"money"—in this story until now. This is a great place to bring it up, because money was (and is) an extremely important consideration in finding the work we are meant to do. Like most people, I had bills that were due each month. I also wanted disposable income so that I could do things

I enjoyed. The fancy term for this is *economic imperative*. The simple version is: I needed cash.

My situation around this time could be explained as follows:

> *Qualifications: College degree (plus half a graduate degree)*
>
> *Career opportunities: Not many (because I would have had to continue studying for several years)*
>
> *Current work: Miserable part-time job (definitely didn't want to keep loading trucks each night)*
>
> *Economic imperative: No trust fund (still had to pay the bills)*

I was glad I had the opportunity to go to college, but for me there wasn't a direct link between college and career. Even though I enjoyed the topics I'd studied, I now knew I'd have to find some other way to make a living. I was also fairly certain that in the ideal scenario, making a living would not involve loading boxes onto trucks in the middle of the night for much longer.

Like a lot of people, I stumbled into something completely different from what I'd initially imagined. I had always liked writing and outlining ideas. I had been reading magazines about entrepreneurship and small business since I was a teenager. I also liked music and travel, though I didn't immediately see how those things would be connected to anything that provided a livelihood. In short, the skills I had weren't all related to that degree I'd earned, or even to my latent talent at the free-throw line in my driveway.

I started my first business by buying and selling coffee, learning about profit margins and roasting beans as I went along. After a few years, I longed for a new challenge, so I went overseas as a volunteer aid worker in Africa. During that time I began leading teams and facilitating group meetings, a skill I quickly picked up since it was something that felt natural to me.

A few years after that, I returned to the United States and began a new life as a blogger and traveler, attempting to visit every country in the world as part of a 10-year quest. (Spoiler: I made it!)

I now maintain several roles, all oriented around the umbrella profession of author and entrepreneur. I write books, I lead teams and events, and I start small businesses. For me, this combination brings me joy, earns me enough money, and aside from a few boring (but necessary) responsibilities, I almost always feel "in flow." To be clear, not everything has been a success—there have been plenty of failures—but I, too, feel like I've won the career lottery and have the greatest job in the world.

Looking back I can see the path, but I never could have predicted or projected it. As you saw in the last chapter, finding the work you were born to do is rarely a linear journey. But when you get there, it's totally worth it.

THE JOY-MONEY-FLOW MODEL: WHAT WE'RE LOOKING FOR

Now that you know that joy, money, and flow are the three key components of a lottery-winning career, let's look at each of the three in more detail. They may seem self-explanatory, but it's important that you understand exactly what we're looking at.

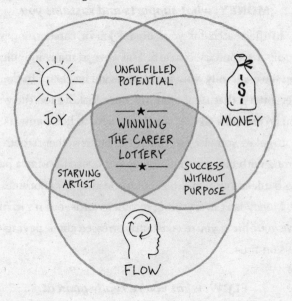

JOY: *what you like to do.*

"Do what you love" may be a tired phrase, but there's hardly a better aspiration for a set of activities that take up to 40 hours a week (or more) from the rest of our lives. It's hard to be truly happy if you don't fundamentally enjoy how you spend most of your time.

This doesn't mean that every moment has to be amazing; even career lottery winners may have to make photocopies and file expense reports. No one can do everything they love 100 percent of the time, but that's not really the goal. Generally speaking, we want our work to "spark joy." If you're not sure whether your current work sparks joy, it probably doesn't.

MONEY: *what supports and sustains you.*

In the search for your dream job or career, money is hardly a secondary concern. You *have* to make a living. If you have a family, you *need* to provide for them. In the career lottery, that ideal scenario we're looking for, the work you do provides all the money you need to live comfortably. If it makes you rich, so much the better—there's nothing wrong with being rich. But even if it doesn't lead to a bulging bank account, it also shouldn't lead to the poorhouse.

Money isn't everything, in other words, but it's hard to love your life if you're constantly stressed about paying the bills on time.

FLOW: *what you're really good at.*

Have you ever lost track of time when immersed in a project you love? Have you ever taken on a role that was paid—but you liked it so much, you would have gladly done it for free? We'll call this condition *flow*: the art of maximizing skill and getting lost in something you're really good at. This condition, like joy and money, is essential to the work you were meant to do.

There are lots of things we all *could* do somewhat well, or even pretty well. Flow work is different. You don't do it somewhat well or even pretty well; you do it *really* well. It comes naturally and easily to you. When you do this kind of work, other people are impressed or even amazed by how effortlessly you seem to achieve great results. "How does she do that?" they wonder.

As is the case with joy, you don't *always* need to be in flow mode. More likely you'll have periods of flow work interspersed throughout more regular periods of work. But just as you want work that sparks joy most of the time, you want to position yourself to be in the place of flow as much as possible.

Don't have a clue what your ideal combination of joy, money, and flow is? Not to worry. We'll be drilling down on lots of practical, specific strategies for figuring out exactly what it looks like for you. The even better news is that once you've found your ideal combination, you'll know it. It will feel like it was right there waiting for you all along. That's the beauty of finding the work you were born to do.

FROM DREAM TO REALITY

When she was a kid growing up in British Columbia, Canada, Angela May wanted to be an inventor. Specifically, she wanted to be Emmett "Doc" Brown, the fictional character from the *Back to the Future* series who built a time machine. For as long as she could remember, she liked to fix broken household items or try to make them more efficient. It probably helped that she came from a family of engineers, but she was just as drawn to art as she was to science. In high school she took both AP science and AP art, and in college she began drawing a comic series that she posted online. The comic series was a good break from the rigorous engineering curriculum that took up most of her week.

Immediately after graduating from university, Angela faced a conflict. A large majority of engineering graduates in Canada go to work in the oil and gas industry, a field she felt was uninspiring. "Sustainability is our generation's space race," she told me. "I wanted to be part of creating solutions, not just propping up an existing industry."

The vision was noble, but as an inexperienced, recent graduate looking for a position outside the dominant industry, she found that the job search wasn't easy. Angela was unemployed for more than six months, living on meager savings as she watched her friends begin working for good salaries. She eventually landed an interview with BC Hydro, an electric utility that was as much a government entity as it was a private company. The hiring process took three more months—government work isn't known for its efficiency—but she finally started her first real job.

As she commuted by train to the office, located in a tall building in downtown Vancouver, Angela felt like an adult.

"I had business cards and a telephone extension," she said. "I worked regular hours for the first time."

Working at the utility served an important purpose for her professional qualifications: after four years, she received her professional engineer's license, which qualified her for a much wider array of positions. The timing was good, too. Even though that first job was helpful in some ways, it also had its drawbacks. First, the process of promotion was highly politicized. Angela saw numerous bosses come and go at the whims of superiors or because of changing political environments. Furthermore, real change was discouraged. In her words: "They wanted us to propose big changes, but then everything was scaled way back in implementation." Angela had the impression that the only sustainable changes the utility wanted to make were those that related directly to financial savings—an important goal, but also somewhat limited in scope.

She was ready to move on, but to where? And how would she do it? "Once you're in that first job," she said, "no one tells you what to do next. There's no road map."

THE ROAD MAP

The whole time she was working at her first real job, Angela had continued to draw her online comic series, and the project became more and more popular. At one point more than 10,000 people were visiting the site every day, and she self-published two collections of comics, which sold online and at conventions across North America. She had seen other comic artists make the leap into a full-time career, but she wasn't sure that's what she wanted. Drawing the comics was fun, and so was connecting with fans and working on the collections, but to do it full-time would have required her to spend a lot more time on business tasks than she wanted. Nevertheless, it was an important *side hustle*—she did it because she liked doing it, and it also brought in regular income along with the satisfaction of hearing from fans. (You'll learn about side hustles in Chapter 7.)

There may have been no predesigned road map for the next job hunt, but Angela decided on a clear strategy to make herself into a more attractive candidate for the job she really wanted. Now a 28-year-old professional engineer, she set out to recast herself. She took night classes, learning new skills and building a portfolio. She enhanced her art skills by learning to draw in a style more conducive to industrial design. She talked to her former classmates who had gained potential connections after working for several years, and she looked for online leads to interesting opportunities.

Before too much time had passed, she took on a job at a new startup, which offered immediate pros and cons. There were only two other people working in the startup, both older men. The job was interesting, but it required hands-on work at a toxic and dangerous worksite. Right from the beginning, this job felt like a step along the way, not the final answer. Eight months in, the contract was canceled and her bosses—the two guys—fired her.

At first Angela was despondent, but then she realized this was another chance to reset. Odd as it was, the startup experience gave her a more well-rounded background after working for the utility. She went on a long-planned trip to Peru and then returned to Vancouver to continue the job hunt.

This time around, she found an ideal position, doing exactly what she wanted. The new job is in her chosen field of product design, using engineering skills to help entrepreneurs design new products and improve existing processes from bigger companies. The firm was founded by two engineers who didn't want to work in oil and gas, and everyone in the office has a similar mindset of sustainability. Speaking of everyone in the office, it's a small company—just 15 employees at the time we last spoke—but it wasn't as small as the startup gig with only two other people.

The small firm has big clients, including household names that make products used by millions of people. The changes that Angela and the others make have positive, sustainable impacts on the environment. In some cases, like a project the team did for medical equipment in Africa, the work is literally saving lives. Lastly, she's paid a good salary and has ample room for advancement.

Meanwhile, Angela continues to update her comic site weekly. She released another collection of comics, her third, and has plans for a fourth. There are cycles to the "career" work and the comic work, she says, but she's getting closer to having the cycles converge.

IT'S NOT JUST WHAT YOU DO, IT'S HOW YOU DO IT

All of the big career decisions you make should get you closer to your ideal blend of joy, money, and flow—and there's an important distinction between the *content* of your job or career (the kind of work you do) and the *working conditions* (how you do it).

To find the work you were born to do, you need a strong match with both the right content *and* the best working conditions. If only one side of the equation is met, you'll always be missing something important. Great work with a terrible schedule ultimately leads to stress and lack of balance. A great schedule or toxic working environment with meaningless or even miserable work won't help in the long run, either. It doesn't matter how late you can sleep in the morning or how fun your co-workers are if you have to spend eight hours a day doing something you despise.

The kind of work you do is pretty straightforward. Let's look more specifically at working conditions.

There are a few factors to consider as you plan your ideal working conditions: schedule, social environment,

MEANINGLESS + GOOD
CONTENT   CONDITIONS
= UNFULFILLED

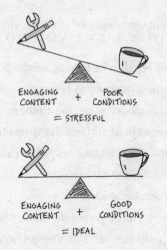

ENGAGING + POOR
CONTENT   CONDITIONS

= STRESSFUL

ENGAGING + GOOD
CONTENT   CONDITIONS

= IDEAL

reporting and accountability, collaboration, and deliverables.

1. Flexibility of schedule. We all want a certain degree of time on our own, as well as a certain amount of autonomy to work the way we prefer. Some people crave total independence and resent any attempt to control their schedule or dictate terms of how work should be done. (Okay, that's me.) Others want some freedom but also like to have a set schedule.

In the story above, Angela found her ideal job in a workplace where she was expected to work fairly regular hours but which wasn't so rigid that she couldn't adjust those hours when she needed.

2. Reporting and accountability. Almost everyone's work is evaluated in some fashion. If you have a boss you report to, at least part of your job involves making him or her happy. And if you have no boss, most likely you have customers, clients, or someone to whom you are ultimately accountable.

Most people want to be held accountable for their work but still have the autonomy to be creative. That said, some people value autonomy more than others. For some, any managerial oversight at all feels like a straitjacket. For others, having someone who looks over their shoulder once in a while to check in isn't a hindrance; it's actually helpful in keeping them accountable.

Angela's first job, a corporate culture where decision making was politicized and challenges to authority were discouraged, didn't offer her the independence to make the difference she craved. But on the other side of the spectrum, she also felt she needed more structure than the free-wheeling startup environment of her second job. Finally, she landed at a company where management was neither rigidly corporate nor completely disengaged, and she found the right balance of freedom and structure.

3. Social environment. It's not just the work that you do that matters but where, how, and with whom you do it. Your working area can be an office, jobsite, cubicle, or shared workspace. You might work from home, on the road, or somewhere else entirely. Once you're there, consider the kinds of interactions that fill your day. Do people pop into your cube or office all day long? Are you constantly sitting in team meetings or conference calls? Some people enjoy the buzz of frequent interruptions, while others hate it. Most important, do you connect with and respect the people with whom you work?

There's no single best work environment for everyone, but these factors are all critical to happiness, and it's important to know your own preferences. Angela never quite fit in at the results-driven corporate setting, nor with the two guys who eventually fired her. But the third job—where her colleagues had like-minded ideals, ambitions, and values— turned out to be just the right social environment.

4. Sense of contribution. We want to be part of something meaningful—a mission, perhaps, or at least something that matters. When I was a kid and my dad brought me to his office, I thought I was helping the astronauts go into space, and it felt awesome. Even if the contribution isn't quite as mythical as landing on the moon, we take pride when we can point to something we've helped make happen.

As you'll recall from Angela's story, her first employers weren't aligned with her mission to use her engineering skills to promote sustainability and help build a better world. Eventually she found her dream job at a company where everyone was equally committed to making a positive, lasting contribution to sustainability and the environment.

5. Collaboration. Do you work on your own, with others, or sometimes one and sometimes the other? This is different from your social environment, because you can be located in an office but still work mostly on your own. Do you prefer it that way, or do you prefer less autonomy?

For Angela, the ideal was an office environment where there were other people around, but she was more or less doing the actual work on her own.

6. Deliverables or metrics. This refers to what you produce over time, or how you measure your work. If you work on a muffin assembly line, at the end of the day you can count the number of muffins you made. If you're a consultant at a think tank, you may measure your progress in number of papers published or recommendations followed.

Angela measured her work according to how much of a difference she felt she was making in the world. To her, that was the metric that mattered most.

7. Security. When it comes to money, it's not just weekly salary or annual income that matters. It's also important to understand how safe your job (and paycheck) is, or how sustainable any other income source is. You could have a gold rush where a lot of money comes in at once, only to disappear without notice. A gold rush is great when it arrives at your door, but by nature it's not sustainable over the long term.

For Angela, the income she brought in from drawing comics on the side allowed her to support herself during brief periods of unemployment, and provided a safety net just in case she ran into financial troubles.

8. Intangible benefits. Not your health insurance or official paid vacation, but anything that you gain by working this particular job. Do you get to keep extra office supplies or make personal photocopies? Is there free tequila on Margarita Mondays?

Angela didn't mention those things when she told me her story, so they probably weren't a huge priority to her. They also probably shouldn't be the most important consid-

erations in choosing the work you are born to do, either—
after all, a soul-sucking job can offer free tequila merely as
a consolation prize. But collectively, they're another factor to
consider when weighing the various pros and cons of a job.

The point is, working conditions are a huge part of finding
that ideal combination of joy, money, and flow. You can't
just find the best possible work. You also have to find (or
create) the working conditions that best suit your personal-
ity and preferences.

Throughout the rest of the book, we'll examine many
different strategies and tactics for optimizing not only joy,
money, and flow, but also all these related elements (and
more) that make up your dream job.

JOY, MONEY, FLOW: A MOMENT IN TIME

The ideal relationship between these variables isn't
the same for all of us, and it isn't always consistent
for any one of us. At different times in your life you
may place more or less emphasis on different parts
of the equation. If you have a young family, spending
time with them may be your highest priority. At other
times you might value higher income or a more challenging position in your career (or both).

You may already know which values are most important to you at this time, but if not, here's a quick
and easy exercise you can complete to help figure
it out.

Action

Rank these statements on a scale of 1 to 5, with 1 being "not important or relevant" and 5 being "very important." For best results, make sure your answers vary, and be sure to have at least one 1 and one 5.

5 1. Enjoying my work is very important to me.

4 2. I want to know that I do my work well.

4 3. I'm in a difficult financial situation or otherwise need to save a large amount of money.

3 4. My lifestyle matters more than money right now.

1 5. Other people depend on me, and it's important that I provide for them.

3 6. I want to be able to do something that challenges me, especially if it's new and different.

4 7. I'm willing to work hard at something I don't enjoy in exchange for a big financial payoff.

5 8. I'm happiest when working at something I love, even if it doesn't pay very well.

3 9. I prefer to work on tasks that I'm exceptionally good at. These things cause other people a lot of frustration, but they feel easy to me.

Results and Interpretation

Add up the scores for questions 1, 4, and 8, then 3, 5, and 7, and finally 2, 6, and 9. Select the highest cumulative score from these three groups.

- If your cumulative score is highest for questions 1, 4, and 8, *joy* is most important to you at this stage of life. More than anything, you want to enjoy your work and do something you care about.

- If your cumulative score is highest for questions 3, 5, and 7, *money* is very important at this time. You need to make some cash, preferably right away.

- If your cumulative score is highest for questions 2, 6, and 9, *flow* is particularly important now. You want to make sure you do work that you're good at.

Remember, all three components are important in your life, but their relative importance might change at different points in your life. Therefore, you may want to repeat this brief analysis on a regular basis, perhaps a couple of times a year.

DIFFERENT FORMS OF WORK

To find your own ideal balance of joy, money, and flow, it helps to figure out not just your ideal working conditions, but also your ideal *form* of work. It used to be that the choices were either to go work for a big company or to start a business on your own, but today the number of options has exploded. Today, different forms of work include:

- Traditional career employment

- Entrepreneurship or small business ownership

- Vocational, manufacturing, or trades

- Military, government, or other public service

- Freelancing or consulting

- Hybrid or nomadic (odd jobs or a combination of different kinds of work)

- Co-working, partnership, or similar

- Part-time, seasonal, or other casual employment

When choosing among these forms of work, there's one more thing you need to keep in mind. Just as there are different professions, there are often many different *specialties* within these professions. If you're a writer, for example, you can write in a lot of different ways. You can be a novelist, a blogger, a technical writer, or a journalist, just to name a few. These roles are quite distinct and have very different responsibilities. And within these roles are also different *employment structures*. For example, if you're a software developer, you could work for yourself, freelance for clients, or work for a company or organization.

In the above examples of writer and software developer, each of the specific roles is quite different, with a great deal of variance in working conditions. The point is that no matter what career you choose, picking the right working conditions can be hugely important in finding your lottery-winning career. And if you're not sure what those are yet, keep reading.

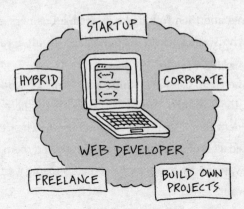

Throughout the rest of the book, you'll learn how other people have used this model to find or create the best possible working scenario for themselves. Among many other stories, you'll read about the guy who made $100,000 selling T-shirt designs through his Facebook account, the immigrant who quit his middle management job without a safety net and then founded a profitable business, and the artist who went back to school at age 40 after raising a child as a single parent.

While their passions, skills, and forms of work differ wildly, the common thread is that each of these people either identified a goal and pursued it wholeheartedly or identified a set of guiding values and followed them clearly. Either way, the first step is the same: to identify what you really want.

It's okay if you don't have all the answers yet. Just remember: there's more than one path, but the goal is to find the best one. You want work that meets the three requirements of joy, money, and flow. The closer you come to your ideal intersection of these three qualities, the happier—and more successful—you'll be. This book is designed to get you there—to be your ticket to your lottery-winning career.

"I had all of these aspirations and interests, but I didn't have any tangible *proof* of what I could do. So I started taking night classes and documenting personal projects. I made myself into a better candidate."

—ANGELA, AGE 30, MECHANICAL ENGINEER

3

Always Bet on Yourself

OBJECTIVE:

Beat the House

Even though the lottery is usually an unwise investment, if you don't play, you can't win. Learn to evaluate risks, make better choices, and create a series of backup plans that will allow you to take the right kinds of chances.

Ever walk into a casino? They're strange, artificial places, and they make for fantastic people watching. Calm, happy music plays in elevators going up, and a slightly different playlist—fast, high-energy beats designed to pump you up for a night of gambling—plays on the way down. No matter the time of day, bright lights welcome you to the betting floor. Speaking of the time, if you don't wear a watch or bring your phone, good luck finding out when to leave. By design, there are no clocks anywhere in sight.

From Las Vegas to Macau, there's one more thing every casino has in common: over time, the house always wins. With a few exceptions, no matter how good a gambler you are, the people who run casinos are better—that is, better at separating you from your money.

We play the game of life, especially the part about career planning, a lot like a roulette wheel. We make decisions based on intuition, and we tend to make the same mistakes over and over. *I'm not sure what to do,* we think, *but this worked the last time, so maybe it will work again. Maybe I'll walk over to the other side of the room and see if my luck is better. Look, a shiny object!*

Fortunately, there's a better way. Instead of playing randomly, we need to play methodically and intelligently. Gambling, after all, is an extremely risky venture, and casinos usually win because they have strategic methods in place for reducing their risk. They can't completely remove the risk of loss, because then no one would ever want to gamble. But on the rare occasions when they discover that someone can beat them in the long term, they bar that person from ever entering again.

Like any game you'd find in those Vegas casinos, most of the career strategies you'll read about involve a certain amount of risk. The key isn't to avoid it completely—because where's the fun in that?—but to develop a foolproof system and manage it smartly, just like the casinos.

AUTHOR RISKS $350 FOR THE SAKE OF A STORY

I stepped into the first real casino I'd been to in years—and the only one I'd ever been in to play. I had an idea I'd been brooding on for several months.

Since I write about taking risks, I try to walk the walk. My goal in this case was to win $50 at 87.5 percent odds. Pretty good, right? The only problem was, if it didn't work, I'd lose $350. Yikes.

Here's what I planned to do: I'd place a single bet on roulette, which offers close to 50/50 odds—not perfectly 50/50, since the casino always has an edge, but close. If I won, I'd walk away with my winnings.

If I lost, I'd double down on the next bet, hoping to recoup the $50 loss and "earn" the original $50 payout.

If I lost that bet, I'd double down yet again with a $200 bet—but only one more time. (Risks have their limits, especially at the casino.)

Remember, in the best possible scenario, I'd win only $50, but in the worst scenario, I'd lose $350. Still, an 87.5 percent chance of success seemed worth it.

So what happened? I approached the roulette table in the Bellagio on the Las Vegas Strip. I put down my money—okay, first I watched everyone else play for 30 minutes so I wouldn't look like a complete idiot—and exchanged it for $350 worth of chips. At first I was thinking I'd bet on black, but then I had a flash of inspiration and switched to red.

The croupier spun the wheel. Forty seconds later, the roulette ball came to stop . . . on a red number. I had done it! After making only one bet, I exchanged the rest of my chips for cash and walked off $50 richer.

> Don't worry, I won't quit my day job—and you shouldn't run off to do this either, at least not with money you can't afford to lose. Still, it made for a fun story, and the $50 nearly covered breakfast the next morning. Casinos are expensive!

A WIDE-RANGING PRODUCTION CAREER

When Steve Harper pulled his car into a gas station in Cheyenne, Wyoming, he had been driving for 1,200 miles with only brief stops to sleep and eat. He was heading west, but the final destination was uncertain. Would he stop in Colorado, cut to the south for sunny California, or continue driving toward Oregon?

All he knew for certain was that something had to change.

For the past several years he'd operated as a freelance lighting and production coordinator in Farmington Hills, Michigan, where he'd grown up. He came to the business the same way a lot of people do—he'd been a musician, and when that didn't go anywhere, he needed to find another kind of work. He'd been left with a bunch of lighting equipment when his last band broke up, so he teamed up with local DJs to work small gigs throughout the region for $90 a night.

The work was limiting at first, but Steve threw himself into it and started learning everything he could about lighting and stage equipment. He requested brochures from all the big companies that manufactured gear, and interrogated the guys running concerts and shows every chance he got.

At some point he received a call from a meeting company that needed production help. They asked if he knew anything about fiber-optic curtains, a new technology at the time. He didn't—but he had read a brochure from the manufacturer, so he was able to fake it until he could learn more on the job.

Steve adapted quickly. After a short period of proving himself (and reading more brochures), he started getting more calls. Pretty soon he was booked for shows every weekend and corporate meetings almost every day during the week. It was nice to see that his new skills were so highly valued, but it was also way too much work. He didn't want to be a manager, yet all of a sudden he had five guys he was responsible for. He wanted to have a life, but his tightly packed schedule allowed for zero free time. One month he was so busy he stopped doing laundry, and whenever he needed clean clothes he would simply stop off at a store in between events and buy a new outfit.

As if these weren't clear warning signs that his life was spiraling out of control, he received a more dire one when he nearly fell asleep at the wheel on the way home from yet another late-night gig. After calling someone to pick him up, he went home and slept for two days straight. When he woke up—clearheaded and rested for the first time in months—he had three tasks to complete. First, he needed coffee. Second, he started catching up on his laundry. Third, he placed phone calls to all his customers and told them he was no longer available for work.

"I just had to quit," he said to me in recounting the story. "I was incredibly burned out and couldn't imagine going back to it."

Quitting so suddenly without another job lined up was a risky gambit, but luckily, Steve had a safety net to fall back on. The years of prosperity had allowed him to build up some savings, which he added to by selling all the gear he'd accrued. Flush with cash, or at least enough to live off for a while, he packed his belongings in a Nissan 300 ZX and began the trip west. He had no idea where he was going or what he'd do when he got there; he just knew he needed to take a big chance to make a big change.

When he came to the crossroads in Wyoming, where he finally had to select a real destination, he chose Portland. He settled in the Rose City and worked odd jobs for a while as he recovered from the epic burnout. He took a trip to Iceland. He went skiing. All the while, he thought about what he really wanted to do with his life.

Gradually the production bug bit once more. He didn't want to kill himself by working 80 hours a week again, but he missed the creative process of designing lighting and putting on a show.

He started making calls and found some used equipment he could lease. Getting back to business was a slow start—an early commitment for a big gig was scheduled for the day after 9/11 and then canceled—but he gradually rebuilt a new roster of clients as word got around about his talents.

This time he was more careful. Today the production work keeps Steve busy, with frequent gigs in New York, Arizona, and abroad, but he hasn't hired anyone and he tries not to overschedule himself. His risky decision to leap into the unknown paid off. Now that he's not constantly overworked and stressed all the time, he's rediscovered the joy and fulfillment he once found in his job.

HOW TO BE A BETTER RISK ASSESSOR

Why don't more people pursue a life of freedom and independence? I don't think it's because they're lazy, at least not most of them. More likely it's because they don't know how. They believe it's too hard or too risky. They're scared. They don't know a clear path with specific, step-by-step actions. But the truth is, most career—and life—opportunities (or at least the ones worth taking) involve some measure of chance.

What if there was an opportunity that wasn't a sure thing but had an extremely high chance of success? If the odds of success in any attractive endeavor were 100 percent, of course you'd step out and pursue it without even stopping to think. And if the odds of success were 99 percent, 95 percent, or even 85 percent, you probably would, too.

Conversely, if the odds of success were meager—only

2 percent or 10 percent—you'd probably say "no thanks" just as quickly. It's when the odds of success are between very unlikely and close to a sure thing that matters get complicated. Everyone's risk tolerance is different, but we all have some range where we'd have to think long and hard before pursuing an opportunity or making a career decision.

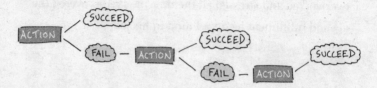

Some of us will make the decision completely scientifically, by trying to determine our precise tolerance for risk. For example: "If there's a 70 percent chance of success, I'm willing to go for it. I accept a 30 percent chance of failure." Most of us, though, aren't nearly so scientific about these choices. Without a crystal ball, it's actually very hard to figure out what the probability of success or failure is. Just like gamblers at the slot machines, we turn to emotion, situational context, and our gut check of whether the decision feels right. Since we don't have all the information, we tend to make decisions in the midst of the "fog of war." Simply put, we don't know what's out there.

Short of that crystal ball, the only solution to this problem is to become a better risk assessor. This isn't as difficult as it sounds. Just keep two principles in mind when considering any big decision: identify the hazards, and don't make decisions based on the fear of missing out.

1. Identify the hazards.

If you're the worrying type, here's one time when the tendency to worry can help you. Even if you're not, take a few minutes to list out everything that can go wrong with any potential change, risk, or opportunity. In many cases, you'll discover that the worst possible hazards are neither life-threatening *nor* likely to occur. Even when the stakes are high and the consequences are substantial, just knowing what's out there can give you confidence to proceed, or the wisdom to back away if it really is too risky.

2. Don't make decisions based on the fear of missing out.

Imagine being on the job hunt and receiving an offer immediately upon completing your very first interview. Odds are you'd feel flattered and maybe a bit proud. But you also might wonder if this opportunity was best, or if there was something better floating around elsewhere. This fear of missing out might cause you to keep searching, or at least delay accepting that initial offer.

But consider if the situation were different and you had been to 50 interviews without receiving any offers. Then, on your 51st interview, you get a call from the HR manager offering you a job. Even if the terms are unfavorable, and the job not quite to your liking, odds are that you'll say yes (and you'll probably say it immediately). Nothing else has worked, so you'd better accept this offer, and you'd better be happy about it.

In these examples, the first job might have been perfect

for you, and the second job might have been a disaster. Because we tend to make decisions based on fear or perceived scarcity, we sometimes feel pushed into a less-than-ideal course of action. The more we can make rational decisions based on the information currently available to us, the better we'll become at assessing risk.

THE TIC-TAC-TOE OF CAREER STRATEGY

Tic-tac-toe, also known as Xs and Os or Noughts and Crosses, is a game of perfect information. With games of perfect information, everything you could possibly want to know about the game is reflected on the scorecard. There's no hidden information, the way there is in a game like poker, where the players' cards are concealed from one another until the end of the hand.

When playing tic-tac-toe, there's also an ideal strategy: if you know how to play the game properly, it's impossible to lose. You can only win or tie. If you play with someone else who knows the strategy, and neither of you makes a mistake, you'll always tie.[*] In other words, unlike poker, tic-tac-toe is a game with very low risk.

Chess is also a game of perfect information. There are no hidden pieces. Both players, as well as any spectators, can

---

[*] To learn how to always tie or win at tic-tac-toe, see Appendix 3.

look at the board and see everything about the current position (and relative strength or weakness) of either side. Unlike tic-tac-toe, however, there is no single ideal strategy. In fact, there are literally millions of different ways to win—or lose—a game of chess. Chess is a lot more like life in that winning is less about memorizing a strategy than knowing how to anticipate and respond to the opponent's movements. Though skilled players will often use subterfuge to disguise their specific line of attack, all information needed to decipher the attack is also available to other skilled players, making the game harder to win and thus more risky.

> *Tic-tac-toe: perfect information, ideal strategy*
>   *(easy game, low risk)*
>
> *Chess: perfect information, multiple strategies*
>   *(hard game, high risk)*
>
> *Poker: imperfect information, multiple strategies*
>   *(difficulty varies, high risk)*

In the game of finding the work you were meant to do, much of the information is imperfect. You'll win only if you develop a strategy that can work no matter how limited your information is. Throughout the second section of the book, we'll look at a menu of specific options—all the different ways you can put this mindset to work. For now, let's continue to equip you with more tools to help you manage and protect against the unknowable, unavoidable risks you'll encounter on the path to your dream career.

IF PLAN A FAILS, REMEMBER THERE ARE 25 LETTERS LEFT

Vanessa Van Edwards had a message to get out to the world. As an expert on social psychology, she spent her days developing business courses on persuasion and influence. The business was going well, but soon she wanted to expand her audience. She'd set her sights on partnering with Creative Live, an online platform for lifestyle and business instruction. Vanessa had several friends who'd taught Creative Live courses, so she could easily have asked for an introduction to a high-level decision maker at the company—but that's not what she did.

Instead of connecting to one of the producers or executives at Creative Live, she took a different approach. She wrote in to the customer support email that was listed on the website, making her case for why her course would be so effective.

At first this sounds like a terribly risky strategy. Writing in blindly, with no introduction, to an all-purpose email address that probably received any number of random pitches? It was the online equivalent of cold-calling. Surely the odds of success would be low, if not nearly zero.

But you may have guessed that Vanessa was actually quite smart. She gave the message an unforgettable subject line: "Here's how I'll make you a lot of money." In the email body, she included a link to a slide presentation that went into great detail about why her proposed course was such a good fit for the company. As an expert in persuasion, Vanessa put her skills to good use, building a case that made it easy for the executives who eventually saw the email to say yes.

The technique worked. Vanessa's course went on to become one of the highest-grossing Creative Live courses—no small achievement, since there are hundreds of courses taught by experts and great teachers. But that's not what was most interesting about her technique, at least to me. When she told me this story over coffee, I just couldn't stop thinking about the route she had chosen for that initial pitch. It was a bold move, no doubt, but it also sounded unnecessarily risky.

Why not just go through a referral? I asked. Wouldn't that greatly increase the odds of her proposal reaching a real decision maker, instead of having the message relegated to the spam folder or deleted by an intern?

Her answer was interesting. She told me she had purposely wanted to build support for her course throughout the whole company, not just in the executive suite. She was seeking true partnership in the project and wanted the people on the front lines to know about her. (A senior producer for Creative Live confirmed that this is exactly what happened: "We saw Vanessa's email go through the ranks, being passed around from department to department.")

Still, though, I persisted—why take the risk of rejection in the first place?

To this question, Vanessa had another quick answer: "Oh, I thought about that. If the cold pitch didn't work as I hoped, I would have gone to the referral network." That's when I understood: there *wasn't* actually any risk. Because her initial approach had only been her plan A, she had a whole suite of contingency plans ready and waiting in the event that plan A failed. In other words, even though the cold pitch was her optimal scenario, she also wasn't banking on it. If it didn't pan out, she'd simply change tactics.

When I was starting out in business, I used to say things like, "Screw the backup plan! Backup plans are for wimps." But now I know that this isn't usually the greatest idea. Backup plans don't make us wimpy; they actually allow us to take on more risk.

HOW TO MAKE A BACKUP PLAN: THE "IF THIS, THEN THAT" METHOD

Programmers and accountants use "if-then" statements to tell computer programs how to process information. If a certain action proves true, then another action is executed. "If-then" logic also forms the basis for deductive reasoning in everyday life:

> *If you turn off the faucet, then the water will stop running.*
>
> *If you walk outside without an umbrella, then you will get wet.*
>
> *If you drink a lot of coffee, then you will feel awesome.*

In programming, good coders try to create fail-safe options in case something doesn't go as planned. For example, Tokyo city planners use this method to figure out how to reroute commuters with the least amount of hassle and delay if a subway line goes down.

You can apply this kind of "if this, then that" thinking to your career planning. Consider Vanessa's example of cold-pitching the bottom rung of the company instead of going straight to the top via a referral.

> *Goal: Get everyone at the company excited about the course.*
>
> *Plan A: Pitch at the bottom and hope it moves to the top.*
>
> *Plan B: Ask for a referral.*

Here's what her "if-then" equation might have looked like:

> *If pitching at the bottom gets everyone at the top excited about the course, then stop and celebrate.*
>
> *If pitching at the bottom doesn't get everyone at the top excited about the course, then proceed with asking for a referral.*

The next time you take on a potentially risky gambit or endeavor, sit down and sketch out your own "if-then" equation. Remember, there can *always* be a backup plan. If plan A fails, you have 25 letters left.

TAKE OUT A CAREER INSURANCE POLICY

If you have a smoke detector in your home, it's probably a good idea to make sure the batteries work. If you have children or other dependents, you may want to take out a life insurance policy in case something happens to you. And no matter your household situation, it's usually a good idea to maintain an emergency savings fund of at least three months' worth of expenses. These are just three examples of common security measures people use to protect themselves in the event of death, disaster, or just bad luck.

But security isn't only about money; it's also a feeling. Just as you should take actions to create tangible security, like the savings fund, you should also work to develop the feeling of security that will allow you to take on more risks in the search for your lottery-winning career.

You can do this by developing "career insurance," in the following ways.

Have more than one source of income. Even if you don't want to be an entrepreneur or real estate mogul, having regular income from more than one paycheck is often the simplest and best way to reduce risk. Later in the book, we'll explore the idea of a "side hustle," where you create additional income sources while still working a primary job.

Keep expenses lower than your income. There's an old proverb about happiness: if your income exceeds your expenses, you'll be happy, no matter how much money you make. By the same token, if your expenses exceed your income, you'll be unhappy, also regardless of how much cash is coming in. This may be an oversimplification, but keeping an eye on what you spend in relation to what you earn is solid advice. When your income increases, you tend to spend more—and that's not necessarily a bad thing. The key is to make sure you don't spend more than what's coming in.

Maintain good relations with everyone. Long ago, Stephen Covey wrote about the concept of "emotional bank accounts," where you make ongoing deposits in people's lives by being friendly, helpful, and available. Because relationships are always your greatest asset, take time to regularly evaluate how you can be a better friend and colleague.

By the way, the consistent use of online social media can help you connect with friends and colleagues. Social media on its own is hardly a security plan, but it's not usually good to be a monk online if you want to advance in a career. Don't open profiles on a bunch of sites that you won't keep updated; it's usually better to maintain an active profile in a couple of places. (Read more about effective social media use on pages 214–215.)

PICK THE RIGHT NUMBERS

Steve Harper's competence helped him become the go-to guy for major events, even after he made the risky move of dismantling his production business without any plans for what to do next. And because he'd squirreled away some cash by spending less than he earned when he was working around the clock, he had the financial safety net that allowed him to take time off to decide where his next road would lead. He was smart and creative, but he was also highly reliable—traits that don't always go together in the entertainment world.

Vanessa Van Edwards made a bold move when she ignored the conventional wisdom of getting an introduction before pitching. She was lucky and the gamble paid off. But even if it hadn't, she would have gone straight on to plan B and probably still would have ended up a winner.

How do you become luckier? An old idea suggests that luck is predictable, and to have more of it, you should take more chances. Let's modify this a bit: to be luckier, take *better chances*. Remember, it's not just a numbers game. It's about managing your risk by picking the right numbers in the first place.

"If you want to create any sort of art, you have to do the work, and you have to do it for you first. There's no point sitting around telling the 'one day I will' story. I did that for way too long. First step is turning up to bat. My mantra became: done is better than perfect."

—LEONIE, AGE 47, ARTIST

4

Prison Break 101

Master the Right Skills

Breaking out of prison—whether a real one or one surrounded by cubicle walls—will force you to think differently and use a varied set of tools. Most universities do not award degrees in escapology, and even if you're leaving from the corner office, no one will hand you a key to freedom. Just as in prison, you'll need to make one yourself.

Daniel Vlcek had an idea to do something nice for the crew of 50 people he supervised at a property management company in Colorado. At a budget meeting attended by his boss and other managers, he asked for $2,000 to purchase pizza and ice cream a couple of times a year for a Friday afternoon party.

Absolutely not, his boss told him. *We just can't afford that.*

Daniel knew that this wasn't true: the company was highly profitable and had a $1 million annual payroll. Two thousand dollars was a small price to pay as a reward for his crew, who worked hard during the busy tourist season.

This conversation was the latest in a series of frustrating encounters he'd had with the boss. The next day he marched into her office with a resignation letter and a bold statement: "I have a great idea that will help us save money. I quit."

Even as the words flew out of his mouth, Daniel wasn't necessarily planning to leave *right then*. He thought that the threat of resignation, offered as an act of solidarity on behalf of his crew, would garner respect and cause the boss to change her mind. Unfortunately, that's not how it turned out. She accepted his resignation without objection. He then got in his car and drove down to the lake—where he did his best thinking—to try to figure out what to do next.

Daniel had immigrated to the United States from the Czech Republic more than 10 years earlier. He'd trained as an electrician and earned a master's degree in marketing, but he didn't speak English upon arrival in Colorado. He took a housecleaning job while he was learning, and over time he was repeatedly promoted until he was put in charge of the work crew—but he knew that working for someone else, even in a managerial position, wasn't the ultimate goal.

Around this time, two other things happened that shaped his future. A college student who worked a summer job at the company went back to school, and before leaving he presented Daniel with a book about leadership. At first Daniel thought the book was an insult—"Maybe he was trying to tell me I need help"—but once he cracked it open, he was intrigued.

The goal of growing as a leader tied into something else he knew he wanted: freedom and flexibility. The owner of the company had recently taken off for a few weeks in Arizona, with nothing on the agenda except playing golf. "He put his hand on my shoulder," Daniel told me, "and said, 'Good job.' Then he hopped in his Porsche and drove off." To Daniel, the ability to drive off to play golf whenever he wanted sounded like a pretty nice life.

The point for Daniel wasn't the nice car or the fancy golf club membership but the *freedom to choose*. He wanted that ability, too—and he also wanted to serve people better than he felt the company was doing.

For a few weeks after losing his job, he stayed busy around the house, but he didn't accomplish much. Finally, he worked up his courage and walked across the street to visit a neighbor. The neighbor owned a rental property, and Daniel offered to shovel the snow, clean the house, or do whatever else she needed in exchange for a few extra bucks. It was a small job and not much income—but she agreed, and the positive response was empowering.

Invigorated by the small success, he decided to kick-start the business idea he'd had tucked away in the back of his mind: to manage rental properties. He got the addresses of a hundred local property owners and hand-wrote a hundred postcards, offering his services. "It took forever," he said, "but I had plenty of time."

Just a single response came back, but it arrived with a contract for services. He had a client!

Reflecting later, Daniel did the math on the handwritten postcard experiment. A return on investment of 1 percent isn't usually that great, but he had gone from zero to something. In short, he was happy.

Even though he still had time on his hands, he decided not to hand-write another hundred cards. For his next attempt at soliciting clients, he got the phone numbers of a different group of property owners and sent each of them a text message. Daniel was averse to cold-calling but figured that a quick text message wouldn't hurt.

This campaign led to two more clients, and he stepped back to evaluate further. In the space of a couple of months, he had built his projected annual income to $27,000. While this sum isn't a huge amount for the pricey ski towns of Colorado, Daniel thought it was fantastic for someone just getting started in business.

Even better, it afforded him the flexibility and freedom that he'd always wanted. A father of three, Daniel began scheduling his days around his kids, getting up early to work, taking them to school before another work session, and then bringing them to the ski slopes from two to four most afternoons. As a lot of busy business owners have found, he wasn't necessarily doing less work, but he was doing *better* work, and he was doing it on his terms.

A year later, he had a full client roster and had begun to hire other people to help out. His long-term aspiration is to own a hotel, but if that doesn't happen for a while, he's not worried about it. "Life is 1,000 percent better," he told me. "I'm glad my boss didn't want to buy pizza for the crew, because now I can do it myself." First the first time in his career, he truly felt like a free man.

YOU'VE BEEN IMPRISONED. WHAT DO YOU DO?

These days, Alcatraz Island is a tourist trap, located an expensive ferry ride from Fisherman's Wharf in San Francisco. For the low price of $45—likely more by the time you read this—you can visit the island where Al Capone was once held captive and learn about its history as a federal prison.

But before it was decommissioned in 1963, getting into Alcatraz required more than your credit card payment and a photo ID. You had to be a hardened criminal considered at high risk of attempting escape to be sent there, usually for a long sentence with no hope of parole. The prison was considered escape-proof, and you probably know what happened next. Just as the *Titanic* was the unsinkable ship that sank in the Atlantic, Alcatraz was the impenetrable prison that served as the setting for one of the greatest escapes in prison history.

On the night of June 11, 1962, three prisoners decided to check out of Alcatraz early. They'd spent the previous year using spoons to dig holes in the walls of their cells, which conveniently led to a service corridor. After finishing the big dig, they set out for sea on an inflatable raft constructed with contact cement and raincoats. They were gone for nearly eight hours before anyone noticed, and were never recaptured.

What if *you* were imprisoned on Alcatraz Island—and what if the situation were even worse? Consider the ultimate bad-news scenario: You've been condemned to life in prison for a crime you didn't commit. There is no appeals process. The clock is ticking and you have only two choices. You can accept your fate and pay for someone else's crime, or you can try to escape. Surely you'll try to escape! But how?

Since you're innocent, you may not be highly experienced in a life of crime. But because you have plenty of time in prison to think, you spend your days devising an escape plan. The first thing you notice is that your plan requires the use of multiple and diverse skills. Maybe your business degree from days of old could earn you a soft job in the administrative wing, which would allow you to gather resources and familiarize yourself with every possible path out of prison. You might then need to secretly copy a key using prison soap and whatever else you have sitting around your cell, thus requiring the reactivation of long-forgotten skills from your days as an Eagle Scout.

You might also have to employ various social skills, doing whatever you can to get a guard on your side, or at least to understand the guards' patterns and routines. You hope that you won't have to use violence—you're just trying to leave!—but you should probably read up on some martial arts so you'll be ready to defend yourself if attacked.

The point is that breaking out of prison, whether a real one or the career equivalent surrounded by cubicle walls, will force you to think differently and use a varied set of skills and tools. Most universities do not award degrees in escapology, and even if your prison is a corporate one, no one will hand you a key to freedom. Just as in prison, you'll need to make one yourself.

THE ART OF SKILL TRANSFORMATION

After having his resignation letter unexpectedly accepted, Daniel was suddenly unemployed and adrift. He sat by the lake and thought about his dreams and aspirations, but he also thought about what he was good at. That combination, ultimately, is what led him to his answer.

In working with thousands of people who've successfully broken out of prison, I've noticed that they are best positioned for success when they focus not just on improving their skills but on improving the *right* skills. They also tend to be acutely aware of two important facts. One is that *everyone's an expert at something.* Often, the "something" has nothing to do with what you went to school for or even what you've been doing for however many years you've been working away at a job. Everyone has another skill or fountain of knowledge, perhaps hidden away or currently unused, that can be uncovered and developed in pursuit of a different (and more profitable) career goal.

The second important fact is that *if you're good at one thing, you're probably good at something else.* Even though your formal qualifications may not be the most relevant in the search for freedom, you've probably gained skills along the way that can be repositioned or redeployed. Qualifications show that you can follow directions (good job!). But merely following directions rarely leads to freedom. Skills show that you can get something done, and they are the keys to finding success and happiness in your post-jail life.

Finding freedom requires you to abandon the lines of reasoning that got you thus far. That's where mastering the right kind of skills comes in.

THE SELF-TAUGHT YOGA INSTRUCTOR

Today, it's easier than ever to self-learn the skills you need to get ahead in your career. Consider this unconventional story from a source who requested anonymity:

> "I'd been a personal trainer, so I knew a lot about the body. But I didn't know much about yoga, and the idea of doing a 200-hour certifica-

tion course wasn't appealing. Instead, I turned to my local DVD rental store—this was back when such things existed. I went in and rented every yoga DVD I could find. Then I turned to Amazon.com and ordered another dozen video sets. I spent the next week watching every one of them and taking careful notes on terminology and poses.

"That was the extent of my training. I started teaching the following week, and entered the studio trying not to show my nervousness. But it was fine! My first hour of teaching went well, and I kept going for three sessions a day, five days a week. I've won awards for my teaching, and our studio is jam-packed. Funny enough, people have asked me to train them. Whenever they ask, I remember that trip to the video store. It always makes me smile."

Lesson: there's often more than one way to do a job or obtain the qualifications you need.

UNDERSTANDING AND REPOSITIONING YOUR EXISTING SKILLS

In any good prison break movie, there's usually a star and a supporting cast of characters. The star—who is innocent, of course—is joined by a motley crew of accomplices who all pitch in to help (and sometimes hinder) the hero's attempt to break out. Typically, each accomplice has a particular skill. There's the toolsmith who works in the electric room and can fix anything. There's the guy with the degree in pharmacology who can obtain sleeping pills for the night watchman's coffee. There's the short, small guy who can wedge himself into narrow spaces.

Most of these specialized skills and abilities are not interchangeable, nor are they easily learned. If you don't know how to hotwire the prison's electric grid to turn off the lights in the guard tower, you're probably not going to master this ability in a short period of time. For most people, access to a trove of pharmaceuticals is hard to come by. And being short and small is a matter of genetic destiny, not something you can simply will yourself to become.

So before worrying about upgrading your skills and adding new ones (more on this in a bit), it pays to understand what your existing skills are.

Entire books, tests, and courses are designed to help you identify and inventory the things you are good at. But why make it so complicated—you know yourself, right? Here's a simple alternative.

1. Make a list of things you do well. *Create an inventory of all the things you know how to do. This list can include:*

- Skills you acquired in college, university, or other higher education

- Skills you acquired from a parent or other role model
- Skills you acquired through the course of your work or career
- Skills you acquired on your own, whether by reading books or articles, by taking an online class, or through pure trial and error

In Chapter 2, you learned about Angela, the engineer. Angela was good at product design and figured out how to put her skills toward helping to improve the environment at a forward-thinking company. In Chapter 3, you learned about Steve Harper, the production coordinator. Steve learned early on that he really liked doing sound and lighting design for concerts and shows, and built a successful business around it. Each of these skills is valuable and somewhat unique. Even if your skills aren't quite as specialized, the key is to make sure you have a simple inventory of them.

2. Write down at least one thing you hate doing and aren't good at. *Just as breaking out of jail requires us to know our skills to execute a successful prison break, it's also important to be in touch with our weaknesses. For example, if you're hopeless with technology, trying to hack into and disable the prison alarm system is probably not the best escape method.*

Your greatest weakness will probably never become a

strength, especially if it's not something you care about improving. In my case, I hate adjusting anything mechanical. If you and I are breaking out of prison together, I'm not the fix-it guy.

In short, with both of these lists, your goal is to focus on what needs to be upgraded—and remember, it's not necessarily the thing you're worst at.

MAKE YOUR OWN COUNTDOWN CLOCK

The final years of my dad's aerospace career were not as enjoyable as the earlier ones. It was probably my fault: I wasn't there to help test the space shuttle or pester him to take me to Burger King. He eventually retired and entered a new phase of life, writing mystery novels and short stories. Before he packed up his cubicle and moved to a beachside office, he created a spreadsheet that displayed the number of days that remained until his retirement age.

It soon became a topic of dinner table conversation: "Hey, Dad, how much longer at the day job?" I'd ask. He'd respond with something like, "Oh, I don't know exactly . . . well, I guess I do. Looks like I have 673 days and 4 hours to go." Soldiers deployed on long missions do the same thing, counting down their time to the precise day of planned exit.

If you're in a similar situation, whether trapped in a cubicle, on deployment, or otherwise imprisoned, make your own countdown clock. You can construct a spreadsheet like my dad did, use an app on your phone (there are several free ones available), or just mark the days down in your calendar.

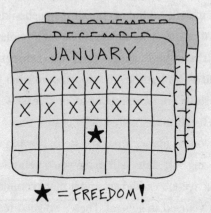

★ = FREEDOM!

Don't have a hard deadline until you escape? Make one. Decide for yourself when "D-Day" will be, and do everything you can to work toward it. However you do it, count the days and prepare for freedom!

IMPROVE THE RIGHT KIND OF SKILLS

When most people think about "improving their skills," they think about things like getting better at spreadsheets or practicing irregular verbs in another language. But for the most part, these things won't help you make big advances in your career.

If the goal is to break free of the job you hate and move into the job you dream of, you want to make rapid advancement in the right kinds of skills. There are two broad categories of these. In your specific field, there are technical skills that relate directly to the work you are hired to do. Examples include a kind of software you should master, or any kind of practical, hands-on skill your job might require. We'll call these "hard skills"—they aren't things that most people will learn, but they're important to what *you* do.

Other skills are more universal, or at least widely applicable. We'll call these "soft skills" because they are abilities that help you no matter what you do in life and work.

Improving soft skills will make you a better employee, a more attractive job candidate, and a more confident spokesperson for yourself in general. There's no good reason not to improve them, at least for most of us. Oh, and one more thing: for the most part, soft skills are generally not learned in the classroom—they're learned out there in the real world. The good news is that, unlike the hard skills you typically need an expert to teach you how to do, soft skills can be self-learned.

1. Improve your writing and speaking ability.

You don't have to be a professional writer to benefit from writing well, and most people have to speak articulately at least once in a while in their jobs. Being a better writer isn't all about using perfect grammar and spelling (professional writers use spell-check, too). To improve your writing, remember that all writing is essentially persuasive. Make sure your writing contains a call to action. Ask yourself, "What do I want people to *do* after reading this?"

Another hallmark of good writing is simply to be engaging. Even if you're writing a corporate report, there's probably a way to keep the reader engaged. Be succinct and try to keep it interesting, no matter the subject. Infusing a bit of humor helps, as do brief anecdotes and stories. Before sending off an important memo, read it out loud.*

As for speaking skills, one good resource is your local Toastmasters International club (operating in more than a hundred countries). Note that the style of public speaking practiced in groups like Toastmasters isn't necessarily what you'll use in your job, but it will help you gain confidence and learn more about how to present a perspective that gathers support. If there's no club near you, practice speaking up more in meetings at work, volunteer to speak at a community board meeting, or give a presentation at your kid's school—but only when you have something to say, of course. Tell stories to illustrate a principle, and if you're going to be speaking for more than a minute or two, decide on your first and last sentences in advance. The key is to learn to be more comfortable and natural when speaking in front of others.

No matter what type of work you do, being able to craft a cogent argument is key. The lessons for both writing and speaking are: be persuasive, be interesting, be confident, and get other people on your side.

2. Learn to negotiate.

Negotiation isn't just for diplomats and car salesmen. The art of negotiation is about finding win-win solutions

---

* For more help in writing well, check out the book *Everybody Writes* by Ann Handley.

to any problem in or out of the workplace. Some people think that the goal of negotiating is to get the best possible deal for yourself—but that's not the point, at least not at any cost. You want to speak up for yourself and get a good deal, of course, but you also want the other party to leave the table happy.

On a trip to China a few years ago, I noticed that there was a fine line between being a good negotiator and being too pushy. If I accepted a price at the market without bargaining, I was perceived as weak and naive. In China, and in many other cultures around the world, the first price is never the final one. You should always be prepared to make a counteroffer. If I argued too much, however, the merchant would act insulted and withdraw from the discussion. The key to getting what I wanted was to walk that fine line—to be assertive, but not so aggressive as to turn people off. This rule of thumb applies in most situations where your goal is to convince the other person to give you what you want.[*]

To improve your negotiation skills, consider the classic advice from the poker table. It's not just about playing well; it's about *knowing what table to play in the first place.* Clearly understand what you hope to achieve, as well as what the other party hopes to achieve. Play your cards wisely and save your best bet for when it feels right.

---

[*] If you ever visit a Chinese market, you'll notice that merchants also walk the line between healthy profits and stealing from people. They too must negotiate well to be successful over time.

3. Improve your ability to follow through and follow up.

Successful people, no matter their field, are good at following through and following up. If you've ever been to a meeting where a lot of good ideas were discussed but then nothing happened later, you've spotted a great opportunity to put these skills to use. It's easy to come up with ideas. Making ideas come to life is where the real value is.

Writing things down is one of the most basic ways to improve your follow-through and follow-up skills. It's nearly impossible to remember all the things you're supposed to, and the mere act of trying to recall everything with total precision can drain your energy. But don't just write down your action items; you should also give yourself a deadline for actually doing them. Follow-up is useless without the follow-through.

There are lots of different systems and methods for keeping track of to-do items. It doesn't matter which system you choose as long as it works for you.

4. Become comfortable with useful technology.

Economist Tyler Cowen writes a daily blog called *Marginal Revolution*. One of his theories about the future is that the world will be even more divided and unequal than it is now. But the division is not just between the rich and the poor, he says—it's between those who are comfortable with technology and those who resist it. "High earners," to use his terminology, are those who use computers of all kinds on a regular basis. "Low earners" are those who are uncomfortable with using gadgets and software. Those who will thrive in the future, in other words, are those who will have the skills to use technology to make their lives better and more productive.

When escaping from prison—or any job you don't love—improving your "soft skills" increases your value in the post-prison job market and helps you break into the work you were born to do.

DON'T JUST BE GOOD—BE SO GOOD THEY CAN'T IGNORE YOU

A few years ago I started working with a web developer named Nicky Hajal. Developers are an interesting group of people: they are almost always highly skilled, but they also tend to do things their own way and on their own schedule. Also—and of course this isn't always true—they sometimes focus much more on the detailed, technical part of a given task, to the detriment of the bigger picture.

Nicky was different. From our very first interactions, it was clear that he was interested in harnessing technology in a way that would *make things better*, not just for the sake of using technology itself. He was motivated by progress and improvement, and if he didn't know how to do something, he'd simply go off and learn it instead of giving up or reporting back on a failure.

Nicky was also phenomenal when it came to follow-up and follow-through. One time I had a project that another developer was initially going to complete. This person wanted six weeks to do it, and we didn't have anywhere near that amount of time. I had a feeling that Nicky could do it in two weeks, but when I approached him, he surprised me even further with his answer: "Give me three days." Sure enough, three days later he delivered the project in full—with a couple of features that he added himself, "because it seemed like they could be useful."

The point is that Nicky isn't just a skilled programmer (hard skills); he's also dedicated, inquisitive, and a good problem solver (soft skills). And these soft skills aren't just important for coders and programmers; they are critical no matter what you do. When Daniel Vlcek quit his job and ventured out on his own, he already had the hard skills of property management, having trained as an electrician and spent years working maintenance on Colorado vacation homes. What really set him up for success, though, was his persistence in mastering the soft skills, in particular the skill of working with people.

Once he overcame his shyness about knocking on doors to talk to property owners, he found he was good at making them feel comfortable with his ability to handle their entire booking and management process. In fact, the more his people skills improved, the more his business grew, and the more his business grew, the more he was able to enjoy the freedom he had always wanted. Losing his job, he said later, was one of the best things that had ever happened to him.

To sum up:

Professionals with marginal skills: undesired

Professionals with strong hard skills but poor social skills: needed on a short-term basis, but not always valued over the long run

Professionals with strong hard skills and strong social skills: indispensable

People like Nicky and Daniel remind me of something that Steve Martin said: "When you're just starting out, don't just be good—be so good they can't ignore you." If you're reading this, you probably already have lots of hard skills. To be so good they can't ignore you, focus your efforts on improving soft skills.

RESIGN YOUR JOB EVERY YEAR

When you're stuck in a rut or simply not sure if your current job is the best choice, here's an idea: once a year, on the date of your choosing, decide for yourself that it's time to quit. You can do this literally or just theoretically. Every year, commit to yourself that you'll choose to break out of prison and do something different *unless staying the course is truly the best way forward.*

You can also do this if you're going to school. Every year, decide to drop out unless continuing the program is the best option. As much as possible, ignore sunk costs. If you've been doing a six-year Ph.D. program and have two years invested before you realize it's making you miserable, does it matter? Not really. Consider the next four years of your life, not the previous investment that brought you this far.

Whether quitting your job, your school program, or something else, here's a draft statement you can use to make your commitment:

> Every year on [date], I will resign from my job. I'll then evaluate if it's the best possible option for me to continue with another year. If it is, I can proceed with confidence and give it my all. If not, I'll immediately start looking for something better.

If you end up sticking with your current job because you love it, great! If not, it's time to get out of Alcatraz. Either way, now you've made a conscious decision and can proceed with confidence.

WHEN TO MAKE A BIG BREAK . . . AND WHEN TO BIDE YOUR TIME

It's a big dilemma: if you're stuck in a dismal situation, do you make a big change right away, or should you build toward it over time? If you want to leave your job and find something better, should you walk away without a safety net, or should you first construct a net?

In the 15 years I've been working with and hearing stories from those who make the leap without a net, I've heard some pretty dramatic tales. Among many others, I've heard from:

- The inexperienced accountant who mistakenly uploaded the tax returns of high-income clients to a publicly accessible site (he was escorted out of the building and told not to return for any reason, making it an easy choice to move on)

- The guy who checked into a cheap motel for nine days, refusing to leave until he finished a business plan for his new project

- The woman who created a social media sensation by using a series of cue cards to accuse her boss of sexual harassment (she didn't ask for a recommendation)

- The people (more than one) who simply decided to not return from a long lunch break, leaving everything behind, including all of the personal items in their cubicles

By nature, extreme stories like these tend to stand out and get a lot of attention. Most of us feel more comfortable with a bit more planning, though. Fun as it might be to storm out of the conference room, it's generally smarter to take your time and plan your escape a bit more deliberately. If you have the choice, use your prison sentence to plan for a better future by upgrading your skills using the strategies you've read about in this chapter; then use those skills to tunnel yourself out to freedom.

"As I've grown in confidence about what I do, I've become stronger at marketing and promoting myself—skills I didn't know how to use before. I've learned how to be bold asking for information from people who I think are doing it right. And I've become really good at saying no to the opportunities that don't bring me joy, or don't align with my values."

—SAM, AGE 53, QUILT PATTERN DESIGNER

5

The Answer in Your Inbox

OBJECTIVE:

Find Your Thing

When you're trying to win the career lottery, sometimes the winning ticket is right in front of you. The answer to your most pressing questions—and the path to the work you were born to do—may come from the people you interact with every day.

At age 40, Sam Hunter made a big change—she went back to school. She had wanted to be an artist ever since she was a little girl growing up in England. But even as a child, she'd been encouraged to find a "real" career. So after finishing high school, Sam came to America and earned an associate's degree in electronic engineering, kicking off a 25-year career in IT. During this time she undertook a lot of different roles, answering customer support calls on a hotline, helping a healthcare company bring its aging systems online, and conducting quality assurance.

She was detail-oriented and especially good at the quality assurance work. She liked to see what was broken in a process and how it could be fixed. Speaking to customers on the phone was another opportunity to problem-solve, as some people were unaccustomed to receiving technical support from a woman and she found herself having to come up with creative ways to overcome their resistance. Even so, she was doing somebody else's work, and she'd continued to neglect her childhood dreams of making a living in the arts.

After 25 years, she decided it was finally time to do something for herself. Back in school at age 40, she earned a BA in sculpture and an MFA in fiber arts. The original plan was to find a tenure-track teaching position, but there were a lot more MFA grads than there were jobs. After applying for every single opening she could find, she didn't receive a single interview request.

Sam had raised a son as a single parent, and when he was five years old she'd started quilting and knitting. At first it was just a fun way to keep her son in sweaters, but the hobby soon became a passion. Around the time she was finishing her MFA, she'd noticed a big problem: a lot of quilting patterns were poorly designed. "I don't understand why someone doesn't fix this," Sam lamented to a friend one day. "Why don't you do it yourself?" the friend replied.

So she did. Sam designed her first pattern and shared it with friends. When their response was positive, she decided to try sharing it more widely.

I loved her answer when I asked how people in the fabric arts world get their patterns out to other artists. "Everyone says that you have to toil in the trenches until a distributor notices you," she told me. "But that's bullshit. I found my first distributor by calling them up and saying, 'Hey, I have something that you'll like.' That's how I've found every other one, too. It takes moxie."

After landing her first distributor through that cold call, she kept hustling, designing more patterns and getting them in the hands of more people. She created a website with a blog and online shop. She began teaching workshops at craft stores and shows. She negotiated with a publisher to write and produce a book. And throughout the process, she consistently did two things. First, she sought out other people who had been successful in the industry, bombarding them with requests for advice.[*] Second, she kept *making*—developing pattern after pattern, and pursuing further creative experiments to put them in the hands of other quilters and see what would stick.

---

[*] One tip: when meeting important people, no matter the field, be sure you're prepared with specific questions. Many of them will be happy to help, but you don't want to waste their time.

As she rolled out more patterns, Sam stumbled upon an important discovery. She loved helping beginners, and just as she'd been frustrated with the template that led her to create her first pattern, she noticed that most patterns designed for up-and-coming quilters were basic and boring. In some ways it made sense—when you're first learning a new craft, you probably can't take on a challenging design right away, so the other pattern designers kept it simple. But the more she talked with new quilters, the more they voiced a frustration with these simple patterns.

And that's exactly where Sam found her next career move. She began designing and selling patterns that *looked* complicated but were actually simple to execute. New quilters could quickly jump into a project that left them feeling accomplished and savvy. It was a huge success. In the first three years, she sold more than 15,000 patterns, with sales doubling every year. It was also a natural fit for her, since she clearly understood the target market. "I've been the person I'm writing patterns for," she told me, "so I know exactly what they need."

When I talked with Sam, I noticed that she shared a perspective with many people who take joy in their work and do it well. Her face lit up when she talked about helping other artists to stop underpricing their work, a cause she's passionate about. The greatest feedback she receives, she told me, is when she hears that these artists have taken the advice of her campaign to heart. There's almost a missionary element to it—she believes in her work and is committed to helping her peers advance.

ACTIVE LISTENING

In the last three chapters, you identified a number of your skills—some that you expected to find, and perhaps some that were unexpected. "Everyone's an expert at something" is a good principle to keep in mind, and often the "something" comes as a surprise. But even if you know what your skills are, a skill is only as valuable as the extent to which people will pay you to use it. How do you figure out which of your skills are most valuable and marketable? In this chapter, you'll learn a creative process you can use to go from skill to solution.

Here's the core principle: when you're not sure what your "thing" is—when you don't know quite where to look to find that job or career that brings you joy, flow, and a good income—the people you talk to every day can help you find it.

The answer may come from your inbox, whether that inbox consists of the actual emails you receive with the same

questions over and over, your social media feeds, or just the conversations you have with your friends. In other words, the people in your network may actually have a better sense of what your most marketable skills are than you do.

The key is looking to the questions they ask you, the favors they request of you, and maybe even the books or articles they send you simply because they think you'd be interested. When someone says, "Hey, can I ask you for a favor?" and you already know what that person is going to ask, you have your answer. Think about it: if you have trouble updating your phone, whom do you ask for help? If you've been going to the gym but not seeing results, whom do you ask for workout advice? When you're planning a trip abroad and need to find a hotel, whom do you ask for recommendations?

Now think about it from the other perspective. Does everyone ask *you* for help updating a phone, or improving a workout, or recommending a place to stay while traveling? If you look closely, you'll probably find that there are certain types of advice that people ask you for over and over. Whether it's recommendations for books and movies, investing tips, or your thoughts on the latest gadget to hit the market, the advice people solicit from you is a huge clue as to which of your skills and expertise is most in demand— and therefore probably the most marketable.

In my case, my friends know that I visit at least 20 countries and fly more than 200,000 miles every year, so they often ask me for help or advice when booking plane tickets.

It's no surprise, therefore, that I found the work I was born to do when I focused on writing books and helping people travel.

If you scan your inbox and nothing jumps out, there are a couple of other ways to use this technique to get ideas:

- When you're in school or the workplace, whenever you've had to divide into small groups to accomplish a common task, what's typically been your role? Are you the natural spokesperson, the detail person, the note taker, or someone else?

- What do you like to teach or show others how to do? Teaching doesn't have to occur in a classroom; teachable moments can take place anywhere. The point is, what do you know how to do that you like to share with others?

- If you're a parent, what do your kids ask for help with? When I was a kid, I learned that my dad was especially good at writing and formulating ideas. If I needed help with a book report, he was always up for a trip to the library or a review of my bad first draft. He used these skills in his work for NASA, no doubt, but later in life he started writing novels, perhaps drawing on the talents that emerged when he was younger.

For the past seven years, I've operated a small business that originally came straight from my inbox. When I first began to chronicle my journey of visiting every country in the world, I often mentioned that my flights were "nearly free" thanks to frequent flyer miles, round-the-world plane tickets, or other tricks I'd picked up from years of frequent travel. Many of my early readers said, "Hey, wait—that sounds interesting. How can I get those kinds of plane tickets?"

In response, I created a basic airfare guide that I offered for sale at a low price. When it sold well, I created another guide, and then others. Then I started working with other writers and a small production team. The business never scaled to a huge level, but I didn't necessarily want it to. It brought in a good income and the work was seasonal. When I had a new guide coming out, a lot of things had to be done, but at other times I could just let it coast along while I focused on other projects.

As time went on, I learned I could trace the response to new guides based on how closely I followed what people were truly saying. When I got it right, customers lined up to purchase in droves. But when I assumed I knew what was best instead of truly listening and tailoring the guides to what my community wanted and needed, response was tepid. This not only kept me humble but was a good lesson that gets at a core principle at the heart of this chapter: the more we focus on solving other people's problems, the more successful we will be.

BE A MASTER PROBLEM SOLVER

Before we go on, here's one more story of someone who looked to his inbox to find a unique way he could solve a common problem. For years, Wes Wages was known as "the video guy." He had a successful business shooting weddings with his wife, Tera, a professional photographer, but he also wanted to do something different. Word of his talent got around, and he soon branched out into concerts, trailers, and promotional videos of all kinds. He was in high demand, usually booked months in advance, but there was still a big problem: he got paid only when he was holding a camera or sitting in the editing room. Eight years into life and business together, Wes and Tera were now raising two young children. Weddings were full-weekend commitments, and the work for concerts and other out-of-town gigs took Wes away from home more than he preferred.

Meanwhile, he couldn't help but notice that every time he shot an event, someone would inevitably ask him, "How do I learn to do what you do?" Wes heard this question over and over from dozens of people whom he encountered through his work, including everyone from bloggers to musicians to his clients themselves. These days, most people have a computer or phone with a built-in video camera—but as anyone who's ever gone online knows, the quality of production varies considerably.

Wes believed that while you can't replicate the work of a true professional, anyone can make dramatic improvements in their photo and video skills with a modicum of effort. So he created an online video course to answer the most pressing questions he kept hearing:

- How much money do I need to spend?
- What equipment do I really need to buy, and what's optional?
- What's the simplest thing I can do to make my videos look better?
- How much time do I have to invest in the learning process?
- What's the next step I need to take right now?

Wes wasn't trying to teach other professionals; that market was already well informed. Instead, he was trying to help solve the problem of all those novices who asked him questions about how to do what he did (and everyone else who used a laptop to make online videos). He'd already been answering these questions for years, but now he was answering them *and* generating a new source of revenue from them. And the idea probably would never even have occurred to him if he hadn't been focused on solving other people's real-world problems.

So what's the best way for *you* figure out which real-world problems you can solve, and how? Here are a few tips:

1. Solving problems of daily life is usually the easiest and most successful approach.

You can't go wrong by helping people solve universal, everyday problems like losing weight, getting stronger, saving money, feeling better about themselves, or anything along those lines. A business that helps people save money on their cell phone bill is a great example of a profitable idea aimed at solving an everyday problem. Many of us pay a high monthly bill without much understanding of why it costs so much and whether any good alternatives exist. If someone can fix that for us without requiring us to change our provider or otherwise spend much time on figuring it out, it's valuable and desirable.

2. Solving specific, measurable problems is much better than attempting to create huge behavior change.

A friend of mine once spent six months putting together a huge set of resources for aspiring business owners who were struggling with their marketing. When I saw the list of materials, I was impressed. "There's so much there!" I said. But that was actually a problem: there was *too* much there, which is probably why the initial response from her audience was okay but not great. Instead of feeling inspired, people felt overwhelmed.

My friend revised the course to focus on a more specific issue: helping business owners improve cash flow. This was better! She was much more successful with the revised offer directed at one specific problem.

3. To avoid getting off track, always ask, "Why should people care about this?"

This isn't a question you can overlook. Ultimately, your success in life and work depends on it ... so if you don't have a good answer, spend more time thinking about it. That's why the project you'll read about in a minute is so effective—because it forces you to engage with this question in each of the interactions.

SET UP SHOP BY TALKING TO 100 PEOPLE

Shenee Howard was a talented brand strategist who was proud of her work. But in 2011, she was also broke and clientless. Unsure of what she was doing wrong, she decided to start talking to people. At first she pursued the usual course of action, asking for advice from people she thought of as mentors.

Then she had a different, better idea.

Instead of talking to experts in hopes of obtaining wisdom and advice, Shenee decided to turn the tables and talk to 100 regular people, asking them about their problems, with the goal of using her unique skills to find solutions for them. Using social media and email, she offered unlimited 15-minute strategy sessions by phone to anyone who had questions about branding—for free.

The sessions weren't just a teaser for a paid service; she really wanted to know what people's problems were, in hopes of coming up with ideas for how she could help solve them. As time went by (she did two or more 15-minute calls a day for several months), she gained experience and got better at finding helpful ideas in a short amount of time.

Some of the calls did lead to paid work, with the free clients liking her advice so much that they wanted to delve into a deeper set of problems. But even when the calls didn't end with a direct business connection, they often led to strong relationships. These people became an unofficial advisory committee or sounding board. They even gave her testimonials. They wrote about the project on their blogs. And when Shenee later developed paid products, they became her most loyal customers.

Shenee went from "broke and client-less" to product launch for her first course less than four months after embarking on what she called the 100 Person Project. It sold out at a good price, and as she tells the story, "the rest is history"—history in this case meaning that she now earns a good, reliable living and works on her own terms.

Shenee's success story is inspiring, but the greater point is that *you* can tap into the wisdom of 100 people to help you get closer to figuring out the work you were born to do. The key is to use the experiment not to drum up business but to get feedback on which of your skills and talents are most valued—and maybe even test out how much demand there is for the product or service you think you can offer.

Even if you think you don't know 100 people, once you start counting your Facebook friends and anyone you haven't talked to in a while, I bet you *do* know at least that many, one way or another. Just as important, the people you know are connected to many other people who can also help you along.

Here's how you can create your own 100 Person Project.

1. List five problems you've been able to solve for someone.

Do this in brainstorm mode, where you don't edit or censor yourself. Ask: "What are the things people come to me for help with? What are the things I know but other people struggle with?"

As I've traveled and met with groups all over the world, I've never stopped being amazed by all the different business ideas hatched and new careers created simply by finding ways to be helpful. From the woman who started a specialty blog about cooking brown rice ($100,000+ annual income) to the professional dog walker ($80,000 annual income) and many more, thinking about problems and solutions is *critical* to finding work you love that people will actually pay you for.

2. Decide on the name of your 15-minute, 100-person session.

If you're going to convince 100 people to get on the phone with you and talk about their challenges and problems, it helps to have a creative or clever name for your fact-finding project. Even though your session is essentially a coaching call or consultation, don't call it that. Call it something fun! A few interesting names that I heard from Shenee were "Love Intervention," "Power-Up Pow-Wow," and "Clarity Chat." Don't get hung up on these examples, though. If you prefer something more business-like, that's fine. And if you're still trying to iron out the details of what your session is about, don't spend all your time trying to get the perfect name. Always do what feels most authentic to you.

3. Create a short description and an offer for your session.

Shenee's project was successful because it had a clear offer and a defined set of outcomes (provide 15-minute brand strategy sessions to 100 people). As usual, the more specific, the better. One person whom Shenee worked with was good with technology and had identified a need among new entrepreneurs who were struggling with all the different options for online services. He labeled the 15-minute call a "tech intervention session" and promised to help people gain greater understanding of devices and software in a short period of time.

Figure out what skills or services of yours you want to test out, and design the goals and outcomes of your "free trial" accordingly.

4. Create a quick and easy sign-up process, and invite people to sign up.

In addition to name, email address, and phone number (the most important things), it also helps to collect a bit of info from people in advance. What's each person's biggest problem, and what's the biggest thing each person is trying to achieve?

Start with people you trust, and ask them to participate.

Once you have a list of people on board, go ahead and schedule the meetings or calls. Chances are you may find all the referrals you need this way. If not, though, don't hesitate to send the message around more widely by posting it online or asking more people to share it. This is a valuable service that you're offering for free. If you can reach people with a real problem you know you can solve for them (or at least point them in the right direction), they *will* want it.

5. Facilitate the calls.

Use your phone, Skype, or whatever service you prefer to call people at the appointed time. Be friendly, but also keep them on topic. You may be tempted to talk more than the 15 minutes, and if it's going well, you can do that—but make sure it's okay with the other person, too.

6. Follow up after the call (critical).

After you finish each session, be sure to send a follow-up note. If you have the other person's permission, you can record the call using free software and give him or her access to it. Another option is to send a quick recap of the chat along with your suggested action items. Mostly you just want to say thank you. Remember that these people may become your unofficial advisory board, so it's important to nurture the connections.

That's pretty much it. For best results, repeat 100 times.

BUT WAIT, HOW DO I GET PAID FOR THIS?

The 100 Person Project isn't meant to be an academic exercise. There are a couple of different ways to turn it into a paycheck, either right from the outset or a bit later on. Shenee monetized it quickly by offering more in-depth client sessions for those who were interested. After a number of sessions, she gained a better understanding of what her prospective clients needed, and used this data to develop a course called Hot Brand Action.

Far more valuable than an immediate payoff, though, is how the 100 Person Project *helps you to discover what you can offer*. Remember, the whole point is learning what you're good at that other people want to pay for. This is hugely important! As Shenee put it:

> As you start doing more and more, you'll get faster and you'll start realizing what types of problems you like helping with the most. For example, my Shazam Session started off as an *everything* business call, and I soon fine-tuned it into a call that was mostly about getting lightning-fast clarity. People would come to me with what they were stuck on and I would help them get unblocked.

No matter what type of work you currently do—whether you're an entrepreneur, a self-employed consultant, or an employee who's looking for a way to bring in extra cash on the side—if you're struggling to figure out what it is that you do well and that others will also pay you for, consider giving the 100 Person Project a try. You now have both the reasons and the tools you need to launch one.*

THE ART OF THE FOLLOW-THROUGH

Once you've identified a skill you think people will pay you for, what's next? How do you actually transition that skill to a steady paycheck? It all comes down to the art of the follow-through.

A lot of people have great business ideas, or at least they think they do, but most of them never do anything about them. It's kind of like writing a book: something like 80 percent of people say that they want to write a book one day, but less than 10 percent actually do it. (And if you want to write a book, it's not that hard—I hope you follow through with your goal!)

The people you met in this chapter—Sam, Shenee, and Wes—were successful not only because they found good ideas in their inboxes but also because they *took action* by following up on them. As you mine your inbox or conver-

---

* Want to know more about the logistics of scheduling calls, as well as exactly what to say in your session? Get a free script and several examples at BornforThisBook.com.

sations for ideas, what are actions you can take to follow through? A few options include:

- Teach people through lessons, tutoring, or consulting

- Create a product, course, guide, or app

- Design a service that takes a time-intensive task off someone's hands

- Apply this model to your job (see below)

If you're not interested in entrepreneurial ventures, you can still use the answer-in-your-inbox strategy to better monetize your skills at work and achieve greater results in your current job, whatever that may be. Instead of taking what you learn and setting up a lemonade stand or cranking out an online business, you can repurpose it toward working smarter in the job you already have.

Let's take meetings as an example. In most meetings, there's a stated agenda and an unstated one. People are not always able to clearly express their needs. If you can learn to pay attention to the unstated agenda and the unspoken needs, you'll build stronger relationships. If you can help your boss and colleagues *feel better* about their work, your reputation will soar. If you can do something for your customers or clients that goes beyond your professional commitment, you'll be rewarded for it. Whether you're an entrepreneur or an employee, your goal is to meet needs and provide solutions. The more you focus on activities related to this goal, the more successful you'll be.

Shenee's life changed as she made her way through the 100 phone calls. She gained confidence and clarity as a strategist. She strengthened relationships that have stayed with her, years later. She now earns a good living and spends her time on work she enjoys. Would this have been possible without the 100 Person Project? Sure, possibly. But by delving deep into her skills and better understanding what she could offer, she took a major shortcut on her desired path of freedom.

Meanwhile, Sam Hunter built a successful fiber arts business by spotting an unmet need. As with any hobby, there were far more beginning quilters than experienced ones—but all of the existing beginner patterns were boring. Then, with grit and persistence, she hustled her way in the door of distributors and shops. After that, she paid attention to what people wanted and developed the business further. As soon as she started asking questions, she realized that the answer had been right in front of her all along.

"Develop the habit of being a humble expert. Be interested more in how other people do things than in telling them how you are doing it. Your work will speak for itself. I still struggle with imposter syndrome, but over time I've tried to support people as much as possible in specific ways."

—LEON, AGE 47, TECHNICAL EVANGELIST

6

Life Coaching from Jay-Z

OBJECTIVE:

Expand Your Options, Then Limit Them

You might not be facing a dilemma between a life of crime or an endless stream of record label royalties, but you too face choices on how to build for the future. The best method for choosing between two or more viable paths or opportunities? First, expand your options. Then start limiting them.

Before he was the billionaire entertainer known as Jay-Z, Shawn Carter was a drug dealer who worked the public housing projects of Brooklyn. Looking back at his early years, even he seems incredulous about his almost unbelievable rise. "Based on my own experiences," he told filmmaker Ron Howard, "I would have never believed I'd be here today. If I had dreamt it and said, 'This is where I want to end up,' I would have fallen far short."

The streets of Brooklyn in 1986 were a lot different from the gentrified neighborhoods there today. Hip-hop was on the rise, but the environment was rough, with addicts lining the streets and crime wars being waged throughout neighboring buildings.

At age 15, Shawn Carter had two primary activities. One was writing rap lyrics in his kitchen. The other was selling crack in the stairwells of the Marcy housing projects. When he looked to his future, with role models and success stories few and far between, the only real options he saw were two clearly opposing career tracks:

> *Option 1: Professional drug dealer*
>
> *Option 2: Professional entertainer*

Both of these careers were long shots, with success not guaranteed either way. Notwithstanding the legal and moral issues of selling cocaine, perhaps the better short-term choice would have been to continue with drugs. There was an immediate payoff—in cash and tax-free. Status was also higher: in Brooklyn in the 1980s, drug dealers were some of the most powerful (and feared, if not always respected) people in the community. Lastly, being a drug dealer was relatively easy. The young Shawn Carter *knew* how to sell drugs. It was a market with virtually limitless demand, and he had a client base that kept coming back again and again. The status quo decision, and perhaps the most likely one, was to continue selling drugs.

But as we all know, he didn't.

Shawn Carter didn't become a famous drug dealer—and that's a good thing, since most famous drug dealers are dead. In the music industry, while there's no guarantee of stardom, the consequences of failure are usually much lower. If you fail, you have to get a day job. If you fail in drug dealing, however, you go to prison or you die.

But even with mortality risks aside, chances are that none of us would know Jay-Z's name if he hadn't chosen the life of rhyme above the life of crime. He wouldn't be worth $1 billion, he probably wouldn't have won Beyoncé's heart, and the odds are high that he'd be incarcerated if not dead.

Here's how Jay-Z described his success years later: "The reach that this music had for me was unbelievable. Of course luck plays a part in it, but every human being has genius-level talent. There are no chosen ones. You have to find what you're great at and tap into it."

Pursuing a career in music wasn't just about making a better ethical and lifestyle choice. It was also about making the right career choice—the choice to do something he loved (joy), something he could get paid well for (money), and something he was skilled at (flow).

You might not be facing the same dilemma between drug dealing and superstardom, but you can use a similar method of analysis to make your own career choices.

FIRST EXPAND YOUR OPTIONS, THEN LIMIT THEM

Let's assume you aren't considering a career in drug dealing or rapping. But you still may be facing a difficult career dilemma. There's one foolproof tactic you can use, especially at the beginning of a career or even later in life when you're planning to make a fresh start: you can work to expand your options, then limit them.

Jay-Z faced an extreme choice between two high-risk, high-reward vocations. But chances are he probably could have done any number of other things, too—they just wouldn't have been the best options for him. He could have gone to community college, gotten a regular job (i.e., not selling drugs or music), joined the Peace Corps, and so on.

You, too, may have many more options than you realize. You can start identifying those options by listing as many possibilities as you can think of. For now, they don't have to be practical or realistic. Your list may include items such as:

- Continue what you're doing now

- Negotiate with your employer to change your role, responsibilities, or schedule

- Search for a new job in the same field

- Search for a new job in an entirely different field

- Go back to school or otherwise get retrained to learn a new skill

- Begin working on a side hustle (see Chapter 7)

- Go into business with a friend

- Retire to a life of cruising the Mediterranean on a yacht with Leonardo DiCaprio (may not be available to everyone)

Depending on what stage of life you're in, your list may contain even more items, several of which may seem attractive. But with so many options, making choices will then become only more difficult. It will greatly help you, therefore, if you can eliminate some of these options using the Joy-Money-Flow model. Remember:

Joy: what you love to do

Money: what pays the bills

Flow: what you're really good at

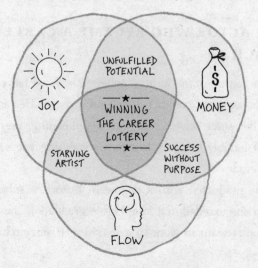

Your first step is to eliminate ideas that don't bring you joy when you think of them. This should usually be the initial decision-making criterion, because life is short and you certainly don't want to do something you don't like.

You should next eliminate ideas that don't have real potential to produce income. This doesn't mean you can't do those things as a hobby, but this book isn't about hobbies. The goal is to make career changes that bring happiness *and* income.

Finally, you should eliminate ideas that you aren't particularly good at, or where your skills aren't unique.

Remember, there's more than one path. But finding your dream career isn't about what you *can* do; it's about what you *should* do. The goal isn't just to find any possible path but to find the path that's best for you.

THE ACTOR WHO BECAME A CAREER COACH

When Laura Simms went to college, she liked her classes well enough but couldn't decide on a major. Her advisor gave her some advice that was well-meaning, even if it wasn't terribly helpful: "Just pick something you can get good grades in."

She graduated with a degree in history, a subject in which she excelled, but long before graduation she knew she didn't want to work in a museum. History felt stale, while drama—the theater—felt alive. She sensed an even stronger pull to the stage after a trip to England, where she met Shakespearean actors and felt an immediate camaraderie. After she returned home, she went to a group casting call for a number of theater companies that would be producing plays in the summer season. The casting call was several hours from home, and after callbacks were posted, Laura was disappointed to see that she didn't get a single one.

On a whim, she checked the board one more time before leaving—and this time her name had been added. It was one callback out of 40, but that was all she needed. She got the role and went on tour throughout the region.

After several years of working in regional theater, Laura wanted to take her skills to the next level. She applied for and was accepted at the University of California's Claire Trevor School of the Arts, which offered a competitive three-year MFA program that included rigorous training and had a strong track record in placement for graduates. After graduating, she worked as a professional actor for several years, sometimes full-time and other times on the side, supplementing her career with a variety of other jobs.

She did TV work, appearing on several well-known series. In time her star began to rise. Yet there was something about the entertainment business that bothered her. "Acting there wasn't just about process," she told me. "It was also about who you knew, who you were having lunch with, and the whole 'scene' thing." The work was good, in other words. It was the culture and working conditions—specifically the need to constantly be seen around the right people—that she didn't like.

Around this time, her alma mater at the University of California asked her to return to teach for a semester, an idea that was immediately exciting. The idea also represented a clear turning point. The teaching gig would be an hour's drive away and during the crucial "pilot season" when major and supporting roles are assigned by casting directors. If she accepted the offer, she'd have to call her manager and essentially take herself out of auditions for a minimum of several months.

This dilemma presented Laura with a clear choice: whether to take a risk with a new opportunity, abandoning the career that she had invested so much in, or stick with a status quo that was no longer bringing her joy.

Sometimes the thing you've done for so long isn't what you need to do next. The right decision was obvious, but fully accepting it took time. Even as she accepted the teaching offer, Laura struggled with a sense of betrayal and guilt. "I had done the acting thing for so long," she said. "I'd sacrificed for my career. I'd missed weddings, births, and funerals of loved ones back home."

She taught the class, but the moment the semester ended she found herself still at a crossroads. After having been away from the entertainment world for a while, she knew she didn't want to go back. The only problem was that she didn't know what she wanted to do instead. Figuring it out required her to go through what she described to me as a wilderness period. This was a whole two-year period, she said, during which she simply didn't know what she'd do next.

Over the course of those two years, she expanded her options by trying a lot of things, and a lot of things didn't work. Among other false starts, for a while she thought she'd be a web designer. She bought a lot of books and dutifully studied, but quickly realized it wasn't the right career for her. The next attempt was to be a "creativity coach," which didn't go over well, either. During these experiments, Laura didn't just sit around and try out different business ideas. She worked to support herself during the transition, either full-time or part-time.

Slowly, she figured out what she was good at. Helping people with creativity wasn't her forte, but helping them with their *careers* felt totally natural. In fact, that's what people wanted—and just as she realized how natural it felt to her, her options narrowed as more and more people started asking for it. Laura underwent training and began building an online profile, leading to more referrals. She started a video series and improved her website.

Once while she was making a sandwich after a coaching session, her husband walked into the kitchen. "I can always tell when you've finished talking to someone," he said. "You have the biggest smile on your face."

It was true: career coaching wasn't just something that Laura was good at. It made her *feel* different than the other kind of work did. It was also something that paid well, especially as she grew her profile and began offering group courses. Laura and her husband had recently had their first child, and the working conditions were ideal. She could work as much as she wanted, but no more, and almost always on her preferred schedule. The time spent with clients was all about the work itself and not about the scene of needing to impress directors or industry insiders. *This* was the work she had been searching for.

DON'T THINK LIKE A CEO; THINK LIKE A JANITOR

I used the Jay-Z story to show an extreme choice of divergent career paths. Be careful, though, that you don't try to literally emulate the exact same path to success. A typical business book or advice column starts off with a profile of a well-known business founder, celebrity, or other highly successful person as the model. The author examines that person's daily routine and priorities, then extrapolates to suggest what you should do. These narratives tell us that if only we too did X, Y, and Z, we too would be as successful as Warren Buffett, Bill Gates, or any other larger-than-life figure. But guess what? The problem with this advice is that what works for Warren or Bill won't necessarily work for us. We aren't Warren or Bill, nor are we Steve Jobs, Gwyneth Paltrow, or any other household-name celebrity. We aren't billionaires with fortunes to invest, and we don't have thousands of underlings at our feet, ready to do our bidding.

Maybe the lesson isn't to do what Warren Buffett does,

for there can only be one of him. Instead, you should learn to do what works for you at this time.

It's all the fault of that old "think like a CEO" advice. You're the CEO of your life, the idea goes, so you should think like a real CEO. But the problem isn't just that you're the CEO of your life; it's that you're not only CEO, you're also CFO, COO, in-house counsel, chairman of the board, and chief janitor. So when you hear "think like a CEO," maybe you need to think more like the janitor or the proverbial mailroom guy.

The janitor doesn't sit atop a mountain and issue decrees; he has to implement whatever tasks he designs. Similarly, your life is not a corporation with thousands of employees, and you're the one who has to live with your choices and carry out your decisions. Also, a life is different from a corporation. Your goals and values are different. Sometimes you need to think like a CEO, but other times you should think like the janitor, the guy who works throughout the building, knows everyone, and keeps his eyes on the pulse of the business at all times.

WARREN BUFFETT'S "FIVE LIFE GOALS" MODEL OF SUCCESS

I've said that you shouldn't attempt to emulate Warren Buffett when it comes to investing, unless you happen to have a spare $70 billion lying around. But when it comes to goal setting, the sage of Omaha has some interesting advice that may apply to everyone.

> According to legend, Buffett once asked a strug-
> gling friend to write down his list of goals this way:
>
> 1. First, make a list of the top 25 things you'd
>   like to do in life.
> 2. Next, circle the top five things from this
>   list. Choose wisely!
> 3. Discard the other 20 items. Work *only* on
>   tasks that relate to the top five goals.
>
> The principle is that you can't work hard on 25 im-
> portant things at once. You might think that the other
> 20 are still important, just not as important as the top
> five. But no—Buffett's advice is to run away from the
> non-circled items as fast as you can. By choosing only
> five life goals, you'll be far more invested in achieving
> them.

EXPAND YOUR BASKETS, THEN LIMIT THEM

You've probably heard the classic advice: "Don't put all your eggs in one basket." When building a life of freedom, how do you choose which eggs to pursue—and how do you fig-ure out which hypothetical basket to put those proverbial eggs in? (Hint: Almost no one knows the answer without a lot of experimentation.)

There are two major, conflicting theories on this topic. On one side, there's the "do one thing" movement, which advocates going all in on your career path, project, or busi-ness. According to this theory, side projects and hybrid forms of work are distractions. When you try to mix it up and do a lot of different things, your attention will be divided and each role or project will suffer.

The opposing theory is the "have it all" promise, which encourages multiple projects and businesses. This theory argues that most people don't want to do the same thing all the time. Just as important, this theory also claims that it's ultimately safer and less risky to split your time among different moneymaking pursuits.

Whether it's wise to put all your eggs in one basket is a great question for debate, because it's easy to argue either side—yet it's not a hypothetical or abstract argument. How you handle these decisions will have real consequences in your life. Without understanding how to choose between competing projects and ideas, you're destined to waver— and continual wavering will *definitely* not serve you well.

Fortunately, there's a real method that will help you navigate the choices by examining the question from the following perspectives.

1. Focus. Are you the type of person who tends to focus hard on one thing at a time? The classic "do one thing" perspective holds that you'll only really "crush it" when you devote your attention to one big project or aim. Do you believe that your chance for greatness lies in forsaking other interests in order to go all in and work toward something with all your heart?

2. Diversification. Do you tend to bounce from one project to the next? Are you notorious for multitasking, or leaving things unfinished? The classic argument of the "have it all" promise is that you'll have more security if your income comes from different sources. The counterargument is that if you try to do too many things at once, you'll spread yourself too thin and end up doing none of them well. According to this view, you could see much better results by focusing on one "egg," or one core business project.

But what if you don't know the answers to these questions yet? What if focus and diversification both sound good? Simply put, unless you are the owner of a crystal ball, when you first start out, you don't know what's going to work. You have ideas and theories, but bank tellers are notoriously resistant to depositing ideas and theories in your bank account.

Could there be any other solution? Yes, there is.

The answer is to start with a lot of different baskets. Try a lot of things. Over time, you discover something that requires more of your time and attention—and that's when you switch to focusing more and more on that one thing. In other words, you expand your options, and then you limit them.

Chances are you'll work on many different ideas and projects, or at least many different iterations of an idea or project, before finding what really works. You may not know what that thing is for a while. Then, at some point, perhaps you'll find it—or at least you'll find something that's truly promising. That's when you make the jump! That's when you go all in. That's when you start taking all those eggs and putting them in a single basket.

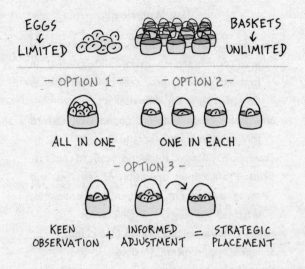

And here's a final piece of advice that's been attributed to numerous people, including Mark Twain and Andrew Carnegie: "Put all your eggs in one basket, then watch that basket very carefully."

CREATE A RESUMÉ FROM THE FUTURE

If you're having trouble finding your unique combination of joy, money, and flow, take a few minutes to consider what you'd like your resumé to look like several years from now. We'll call this your "resumé from the future."

For example, say you're getting started just out of college as a junior analyst with an energy company. The job is interesting, but it's entry-level, so you want to move up and move on as soon as possible. Here's how your resumé from the future might look.

Your Name Here

Summary: Former junior analyst worked hard and contributed to major advancement in first assignment; now seeks greater role as Commander in Chief or similar

Education: Ph.D., Stanford (honorary), Oxford (online), too many others to list

Experience: Changed the world; plans to continue

Skills: Proficient in operation of jetpacks and zero-gravity flight, fluent in five languages, leaps tall buildings in single bounds

Salary requirements: $$$$$$$ (cha-ching)

Schedule requirements: Flexible

Ideal working conditions: A job that provides the right balance between working independently and working with others, with just the right amount of challenge

Perhaps you won't want to list jetpacks or zero-gravity flight on your resumé from the future, and maybe you'll speak only four languages by then. Once you have a few ideas listed, though, your next step is to choose the career options that are most likely to make your future dreams a reality. For example, if your resumé from the future includes an advanced degree or any other training, consider if there's anything you can do to begin that process now. Or if your ideal working conditions involve a role with greater responsibility, don't wait until you're offered the role to tackle it.

It's good to look to the future while you make decisions in the present. When you look to the future you imagine, you can use the present to take actions that make the imaginary real.

Once he found what he was meant to do, Jay-Z gave it everything he had. He didn't do what was expected of him, and he figured out a way to give himself a choice.

Laura Simms found a way of life that best utilized her skills. It wasn't a quick or linear journey—and when the first ideas didn't work, she didn't hesitate to take on another job to pay the bills. Still, she kept iterating and finally discovered a specific type of career coaching that brought joy to her life as she helped clients improve theirs. She increased her options to find this ideal solution, then she limited them as it became clear that it would work.

Your options are not limited to the training you've received or to what you've done thus far. There may be something much better just waiting for you to experiment and explore.

NEXT STEPS: A MENU OF OPTIONS

The next section of the book is all about specific strategies for different kinds of work. Here's a quick summary of the menu items that lie ahead:

Side Hustle: Generally speaking, everyone should have some kind of side hustle. Chapter 7 will help you make more money by beginning a microbusiness, even if you never want to work for yourself full-time.

You, Inc.: Some people want to go all in on their own venture. Chapter 8 will help you take the leap from a small project to a big (or at least medium-sized) empire.

How to Find Your Dream Job: Forget about updating your resumé; most dream jobs are found or created through nontraditional methods. Chapter 9 will help you "act outside the box" and match up with the best possible employer.

The Self-Employed Employee: Hack your job by becoming invaluable to the organization—then use your status to ensure that the job continues to meet all of your needs.

DIY Rock Star: Today's musicians, artists, and writers understand who pays their rent, and it's not the record labels or patrons of old. Chapter 11 explores the new world order of making a living through direct relationships with fans.

How to Do More Than One Thing: Some people find success by specializing, but others prefer to mix it up and pursue multiple goals at the same time. No matter what you choose, you'll learn to craft a life around all your interests.

Winners Give Up All the Time: Real winners won't hesitate to walk away from an unsuccessful venture. Chapter 13 will help you master the art of moving on by learning when to quit and when to keep going.

By the way, I hope you're enjoying the book so far. If you'd like to check in about something you've read, write me at hello@chrisguillebeau.com.

"I was amazed at how great it felt to have extra money coming into my bank account. I kept my day job, but the side project was something I looked forward to working on whenever time allowed. It gave me confidence and hope."

—HASSAN, AGE 42, FULL-TIME ARCHITECT AND
PART-TIME ENTREPRENEUR

7

Side Hustle

OBJECTIVE:

Make More Money

Before we go any further, let's equip you with a means of financial support outside of conventional employment. Whether you want to be fully self-employed or not, you should have some income that independently arrives in your bank account, preferably on a recurring basis. Here are several specific, actionable plans to make this happen—right away.

It was a long and sleepless night for Elle. She tossed and turned through the night, struggling to fall asleep. Actually, not really. She went to bed at 10:00 p.m. and slept just fine.

In the morning she woke up and checked an account balance on her phone. Overnight, $170 had arrived. *Not bad,* she thought.

Six months earlier, Elle had started a clothing business, selling accessories that she created in a whimsical style. After a few failed experiments, she found an easy way to make her goods without taking a great deal of time. For an hour or so a day, she responded to customer emails. Once a week she went to the post office to mail out shipments, and she spent part of the weekend on marketing. The rest of the time, she worked another part-time job while caring for her daughter, who had just started preschool.

Elsewhere, David was hard at work as an industrial engineer, building semiconductors for a big company. Once in a while, from the privacy of a cubicle, he'd sneak a peek at his personal website stats. He'd started a subscription service for fantasy sports fans a few months back, and it was going well. The extra money wasn't enough to live on, but it made a big difference in supplementing the income from his day job. He'd recently paid off some debt and taken a trip to the Caribbean. The future was bright.

Meanwhile, Maya worked for a nonprofit. She gave her all to the cause of increasing literacy for at-risk kids, and she loved making a difference. The only downside was the money. Maya felt rewarded emotionally in her work, but she wasn't well paid. She had a car payment, rent wasn't cheap, and then there were those pesky student loans from her years at a prestigious (but also pricey) liberal arts college.

Maya had always been tech savvy. She built her own website when she was still in middle school, and in college she coded an app for one of her many academic clubs. Working with her sister, who also had a job in the nonprofit world, she wrote an ebook to help aspiring do-gooders learn to use technology better. The ebook brought in $500 the first month and $700 the second. This wasn't a huge amount of money, but it was extra income for both of them, and they enjoyed it. They planned to devote one weekend a month to writing a sequel and possibly creating an online course.

Each of these stories is true, and they're also representative of many, many more people who've found a way to supplement their income through a passion project they develop in their limited free time. The principle: you don't have to quit your job to start something on the side, and it doesn't have to take over your life unless you want it to.

MO' MONEY, FEWER PROBLEMS

The goal of this chapter is to equip you with a means of financial support outside of conventional employment. Whether you want to be a full-time business owner or not, *everyone* should have some income that independently arrives in their bank account, preferably on a recurring basis.

Over and over, I hear from people who talk about the disproportionate satisfaction they feel when receiving income from sources outside their regular paycheck, especially from projects or business ideas they created for themselves.

We'll call this a "side hustle," meaning that it's something you typically work on in addition to your full-time work or studies. You can also set up a side hustle during a break from other work, in a transition before starting something new, or even when you're already pursuing another business opportunity.

Think you're too busy for another project? Whether busy or not, ask yourself, "Do I have the right balance of joy, money, and flow in my life?" If you want an outcome different from the one your current path is leading to, somehow you'll have to find the time. Being too busy may be the new social currency, but the real winners find time to do what matters to them.

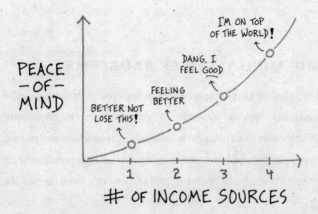

If you're not yet convinced that extra money is good, you're probably reading the wrong book. There are many, many reasons a side hustle can serve you well. Let's get to work on making it happen.

3, 2, 1—GO

Let's say you're persuaded that a side hustle is a good move for you. How do you do it?

First, keep in mind what we looked at earlier: in your dream job, you want to find the ideal intersection of joy, money, and flow—and you'll get there by meeting people's needs and providing real solutions. This principle holds true for side hustles, too. To do that in this context, there are four broad types of hustles to choose from. We'll look at each one in detail.

1. Sell something.

Amber had always been a crafter, and she used to sell her fabric art at the weekly markets in her hometown of Myrtle Beach, South Carolina. But sales were slow and customers were limited. Except for tourist season, the same people dropped by every week. Several years ago, Amber discovered Etsy, the online marketplace for handcrafted items. After posting a few items and getting good feedback, she branched out and soon had more than 300 listings open at once. (It's not as hard to manage as it sounds, since she reuses much of the content for similar listings.)

Amber now earns an additional $450 a month, with very little extra work. As a single mother who works as a nurse during the day, the money goes a long way.

What can *you* sell? Look at what other people are buying. Observe how your friends spend money. Pay close attention, because with effort and experimentation, you can almost certainly find something that will work.

If you've never sold anything at all and really have no idea where to begin, get some experience by listing items on an online auction site—even if it's just old stuff you have around the house. This may not be the best long-term plan (you'll eventually run out of stuff to sell), but it can help you gain confidence (and a neater house) very quickly. See the sidebar on pages 156–158 for some tips on doing this.

2. Provide a consulting service.

Since I first wrote about the concept of becoming an "instant consultant" on my blog and in previous books, I've heard hundreds of stories of people who learned to master a particular skill or body of knowledge, then made money by offering to teach that expertise to others.

My favorite example, one I've mentioned many times in talks and conversations, is Gary Leff, a frequent traveler who created a series of profitable businesses while continuing to work a full-time job as a CFO. After years of helping friends and colleagues use their frequent flyer miles to book extensive and complicated itineraries, he started a paid service to do just that for anyone who was too busy or lacked the knowledge to do it personally.

Another great example is Harry Campbell, a 27-year-old structural engineer. In a bid to make extra cash, he started driving for the ride-sharing service Uber on nights and weekends (more on ride-sharing in a moment). Pretty soon Harry noticed that the hours he chose to work made a huge difference in the number of customers he served, and therefore in his hourly earnings rate. Curious, he went online to see if other drivers were having similar experiences, but he couldn't find much . . . so he started writing up his own observations on the best times to drive, publishing them first on a blog and then a podcast.

Harry's shared knowledge got noticed quickly. There were tens of thousands of ride-sharing drivers just like him, but since the industry was so new, there weren't many sources of independent news and advice available for them. At the request of many drivers, he began offering paid consultations to help them earn more money by "driving smarter, not longer." The business is now *another* source of income for him, even as he continues to drive during peak hours.

3. Become a middleman.

If you don't want to start a service and don't have something to sell of your own, you can sell something on behalf of someone else and earn money for it. This is called "affiliate marketing," and it's a huge, potentially very lucrative business.

Marie Forleo is an entrepreneur who has turned affiliate marketing into somewhat of an art form. Each year she relaunches her mega-popular online course B-School. The course is an eight-week intensive session designed to help women (and some men, too) master the basics of an online business. Tens of thousands of people have been through the program, and there's always a huge clamor to sign up once "B-School season" begins in the spring.

B-School is great no matter how you sign up, but it's grown so quickly in large part because Marie has been particularly successful in engaging with a small army of affiliates, course alumni who refer their audience to the program in exchange for a commission. Because they believe in the program so strongly, many alumni put a great deal of creativity and effort into their promotion plans—and some of them earn substantial income from the results. But it does require time and dedication, proving that you can't just put a link up on your site and expect magic to happen. You have to work for it!

The key to making money as an affiliate lies in leveraging at least one of two market forces: either some kind of technological advantage (better search engine results, for example) or "authority" in the minds of people interested in purchasing something through your referrals.

One of my businesses, CardsforTravel.com, earns commissions upon referring interested readers to the best travel credit cards. It's a win-win, since people who sign up for cards can get big sign-up bonuses that they can use to travel the world.

Depending on your interests and the size of your existing community, affiliate marketing can be a great side hustle. A word of caution, though: my inbox is filled on a regular basis with people telling me about the latest and greatest multilevel marketing program, and these are almost never worthwhile opportunities. There may be exceptions, but most of these programs benefit the people who started them much more than anyone who comes in later on. Unless you've found measurable results that prove how effective the program can be *for you*, avoid these programs and do something else.

4. Join the sharing economy as a provider.

Trends and specific services may come and go, but the "sharing economy"—platforms and services that allow ordinary people to rent out things they own when not in use—is here to stay. A tidal wave of independent contractors provides the labor (and sometimes the vehicles, tools, and housing) for this way of life, and you can be part of it. Most of these opportunities are part-time by design, and many of them can accommodate the flexible hours of your choice.

These next few ideas may get you thinking.

- *Ride-sharing.* Jaime picked me up in his car on the way to his day job. We'd never met before, but I used the Uber app on my phone to request a ride, and a few minutes later he arrived. He had a full-time job, so the DIY driving gig was just a part-time thing. He also had a clear strategy: every morning, he'd leave home an hour early and head to the airport. Pickups from inbound passengers usually paid higher than average fares, and after dropping someone off he'd generally have time for one or two more trips. On the way home from work, he'd spend another hour doing the same thing. He earned an extra $260 a week from this side hustle.

- *Service networking.* Rachel came to my house after I contracted with her using an online portal called TaskRabbit. Earlier that morning I had posted a listing, saying that I needed someone to return some things to a store for me. Rachel accepted the task, showed up right on schedule, and returned the items. After she completed the task, my credit card was instantly charged the agreed-upon rate for her time. I was happy and so was she—and then we each left a good rating for the other person on the site. The next time I logged in, I noticed that Rachel had completed more than a hundred tasks for other users. That seemed like a lot, so I emailed her afterward to ask how it was working out. She told me she was a teacher who worked full-time, but with summers off and occasional flexibility during the school year. In her spare time, she gets paid to run errands for strangers, doing everything from returning unwanted purchases to standing in line for concert tickets. She used all her TaskRabbit earnings to save for travel, and her current goal was to take a long trip to Iceland with her boyfriend.

- *Property sharing.* After years of renting a small condo, Maylene and Charity bought a house that was much larger. Did they need more space? Not really—they wanted to rent out an extra bedroom to vacationers using Airbnb, the massively popular peer-to-peer property rental site. Renting out one space was fun and profitable, but they soon noticed another big need: many other property owners liked the idea of earning additional income but didn't want to deal with the hassles of property management. Maylene and Charity then started a new side project, offering to manage all aspects of getting short-term renters in and out of client-owned properties. In this case, the side project actually expanded to a full-time business.

Of course, not all of these services and platforms may be available in your area, and some of them will probably change over time. That's normal. The point is that all of the people in the examples above are earning an above-average hourly income for their work while maintaining the flexibility they need for the rest of their life. This is huge!

5. Become a digital landlord.

There's an entire industry of books and seminars on purchasing and managing rental properties. But what's the problem? Well, to start, you usually need a lot of capital.

It also takes a lot of time, and many things can go wrong. Unless you clearly know what you're doing, these are three good reasons to look elsewhere.

The alternative is to invest and create digital assets that are cash-positive (i.e., make money) right from the beginning.

	TRADITIONAL REAL ESTATE INVESTING	CREATING A DIGITAL ASSET
Capital Required	High	Low
Expected Growth	Variable	Variable
Required Maintenance	Moderate to high	Low to high

Note: There will always be exceptions, and real estate investing is good for plenty of people who have enough capital to invest. But almost everyone can experiment with digital assets, and unless you're investing your life savings (tip: don't do that), the risk is typically far lower and the timeline to success much shorter.

When I was a teenager, I delivered pizza. The hourly wage and tips were a lot of money for me at the time, but I couldn't live off that job as an adult with bills to pay. The world will always need pizza delivery drivers, but it's probably smarter (and more profitable) to pursue higher-income services like those listed above. With just a smartphone and bank account, *everyone* has access to a better range of income-earning opportunities.

EARN MONEY WHILE YOU SLEEP, SET YOUR OWN MINIMUM WAGE, AND MAINTAIN A STELLAR REPUTATION

Let's go back to the brief stories at the beginning of this chapter. Can you really earn money while you sleep? Plenty of people certainly do, so don't miss out on the party.

If you decide to give it a go, these tips might help:

Set your own minimum wage. If you decide to go down the rabbit hole of the ideas contained in this chapter, you'll likely find no shortage of opportunities. There's an exercise on pages 164–166 to help you decide which opportunity may be best, but it's also a good idea to set a minimum wage for yourself. This will help you decide which options are worth your time and which aren't. Sometimes in life you'll choose to do things that don't pay well, and that's fine—but by design, a side hustle should pay well enough to be worth doing.

Price based on value. If you're pursuing an entrepreneurial solution instead of just hopping on board an existing service, don't base the price of your product or service on how much time it takes you to provide it; price it based on the value it offers. With some exceptions, the amount of time spent shouldn't be the most important factor in pricing. What matters most is how your customers' or clients' lives are improved. Think about that value when choosing a price.

Finally, remember that your reputation is your most valuable asset. Especially with services in the sharing economy, where virtually every site offers customers a chance to publicly post reviews and feedback on your service, having a good reputation (and rating, if applicable) is crucial. Go above and beyond to make sure people are satisfied. There will always be curmudgeons who find something to complain about even if they received nearly perfect service. But any negative feedback or ratings you receive should be heavily offset by many other positive reviews and ratings.

TWELVE LESSONS LEARNED FROM MAKING A LIVING ON EBAY

Long ago in a galaxy far away, I got my start as an entrepreneur by buying and selling things on eBay and other online auction sites. I wasn't the only one—a whole generation of people came to self-employment through the auction site. One of those people was Amy Hoy, a Philadelphia-based strategist who went on to start several other businesses.

Like me and others, Amy found a way to make a living simply by buying things from one location and reselling them in another. Through thousands of auctions, she learned what worked and what didn't. She developed the guidelines below to help people who are hoping to do something similar. (I used most of them, too, but she did a better job of writing them down, so we're going with her list. Thanks, Amy!)

- Start with a very low starting bid (like 99¢). Higher starting bids result in less bidding frenzy; low bids get more people involved and create a sense of adventure and hope.

- Skip the reserve price, or if you have one, tell people what it is—nothing discourages bids like a mystery line bidders can't see and don't know if they'll be able to cross.

- The more photos, the better; it doesn't matter if they don't show anything "new."

- Even if it's a mass-produced item, include photos of the specific one you're selling.

- If you have many of the same item, stagger the listings over time.

- Talk about the item, how it's used, why it's useful, why it's a good choice, and even why it *wouldn't* be the perfect choice.

- Make the listing personal and personable. Talk about why you have the item; if it's a product category with a lot of fraud (e.g., camera equipment), talk about how long you've had the item, why you're selling it, and when you'll ship it.

- Tell a story about how buyers could use and enjoy that item in their lives. Will the Noguchi-style rice paper lamp give their room a sophisticated, global flair? Tell them!

- Always include measurements, age, maker, and any other specific details.

- Always use the terms (especially in the search fields) your buyers value and are likely to use. You have no idea how many people will call something "art" and not an "oil painting" or a "landscape."

- If there's a flaw, call it out explicitly and in great detail and describe how it does or does not affect the item.

- Be scrupulously honest at all times.

Note: As with other tactics and markets, eBay may not be available where you live, or it may be less relevant by the time you read this. The general rules still apply.

GOLD RUSH 101

Back in the days of the original gold rush, aspiring prospectors hopped trains to California in hopes of striking it rich. Many failed, but some made it. Modern equivalents of gold rushes still come along, and these days they tend to be easier to spot. They also require much less investment and risk—no need to sell everything you own and hop a train.

Benny Hsu, whose story you'll read in more detail in the next chapter, earned more than $100,000 by designing T-shirts and selling them through Facebook ads. Thanks to a new technology and a lot of creative effort, he never had to stock a single shirt—another company did that for him, leaving him free to focus entirely on design.

In Vancouver, Canada, a creative entrepreneur founded Pirate Joe's, a grocery store reseller dealing entirely in products purchased an hour away and across the U.S. border in Bellingham, Washington. Many Vancouverites are fans of Trader Joe's products, which have a reputation for good quality and low prices, but the store has no Canadian presence. Mike Hallatt, the founder, regularly makes south-of-the-border grocery store runs to purchase tens of thousands of dollars' worth of product. It's not illegal, but Trader Joe's is still so afraid of the competition that they're trying to shut him down. (Enjoy the gold rush while it lasts, Mike.)

I once had my own gold rush in online advertising. While experimenting with a side business I had started when I was volunteering as an aid worker in West Africa, I figured out a trick so that I could consistently earn more money than I spent by purchasing ads on Google and sending the traffic to a lead-generation site that paid me on commission.

Alas, the possibilities weren't infinite. I could regularly spend $300 and make $350 (for a $50 profit), and on some days I could spend $1,000 and make $1,200 (for a $200 profit), but I couldn't go much higher than that. Still, it was great to be able to spend one amount of money at night and wake up to a larger amount of money in the morning. After a year, the opportunity disappeared as other people figured it out and crowded the market, but before that happened I was able to save the profits and use them to pay for an expensive graduate school program.

Opportunities are always around us, and when one gold rush door closes, another opens. Walk through the open door!

TO FIND A GOLD RUSH, DON'T THINK DIFFERENT, THINK BORING

A lot of people get stuck in the search for a "big idea." But as you saw in Chapter 5, you don't necessarily need a big idea to make big profits. You need a *helpful* idea. Consider the guy who invented the cupholder. Granted, it's not as sexy as making the latest smartphone model. But if you're driving along with a beverage, that cupholder sure comes in handy.

Consider as well some of the examples you've seen in this chapter. Harry Campbell, the ride-share guy, provided profitable tips to new drivers seeking to be more effective. Mike Hallatt founded Pirate Joe's in Canada to import specialty groceries that he knew there was a market for. Again, *being helpful* is the highest value.

These qualities are good signs of a potential gold rush:

- A big, untapped market

- A new technology or advancement that a lot of people don't know how to use or participate in

- Confusion or uncertainty over how to participate in the new thing

- Something people want but can't get ("illegal" groceries from across the border)

- Something that is perceived as scarce or involves FOMO (the fear of missing out)

Remember, always strive to meet needs and solve problems. Also, when you find a possible gold rush, strike quickly. Begin your experiment even when you aren't sure what will happen. If it works, you can always improve it. If it doesn't work, well, you haven't invested much time and can easily move on.

19 DAYS TO HUSTLE: A SUGGESTED TIMELINE

When you're launching your first side hustle, it can be tricky to figure out how to start. Here's a suggested timeline to get you going. By spending one hour a day for 19 days, you'll be off the ground before a month has gone by.

Day 1: First things first! Decide what your side hustle will be. What skills will you utilize? What passion will you tap into? What problem will you solve?

Day 2: What's the deliverable? Make a decision: will this be a product, a service, or some kind of hybrid? How will you make money off your side hustle?

Day 3: Think about the ideal customers or clients for this idea. Who are they and what are their struggles? If you had five customers or clients, what would they all have in common?

Day 4: Set a budget. Determine all costs necessary, and keep them as low as possible.

Day 5: Write down three key benefits for your new side hustle. This is particularly important, because the benefits you offer matter much more than any other details or features.

Day 6: Decide how much you'll charge for your offer.

Day 7: Set up a simple, one-page website. No need to make it complicated or fancy; for a quick guide on how to get a website in less than an hour, visit BornforThisBook.com.

Day 8: Write a simple sales page for your website. Again, it doesn't need to be complicated; just think about what you're offering and how it will help people. Oh, and tell them what they need to do to purchase or sign up.

Day 9: Write the "Frequently Asked Questions" section for your website. Think about what questions *you'd* have upon encountering your offer for the first time. What would you want to know?

Day 10: Add a PayPal button (or other checkout process) to your one-page website. Remember, if you don't have a way to get paid, it's called a hobby, not a business.

Day 11: Alternatively, offer to invoice clients for your service. If you choose this option, make sure there's a clear way for them to commit to payment before you do a bunch of work for them.

Day 12: Show your draft project to three people and ask for feedback. For best results, don't just ask friends; ask people who fit the background or profile you identified on day 3. Ask for their unfiltered opinion and make sure they tell you about anything that isn't immediately clear to them.

Day 13: Launch! Publish your offer or simple website. Congratulations—but don't celebrate too much, because there's more to be done.

Day 14: Tell your friends. Let them know what you're working on and how they can help spread the word.

Day 15: Tell other people you know—friends of friends, colleagues, former classmates. Don't try to sell them directly; just ask them to refer your project on if they know anyone who might be a good fit for it.

Day 16: Mention your offering on social media. Again, don't try too hard to sell, but do show people what you've made.

Day 17: Ask your first customer or client to share his or her honest opinion. What did that person like, and how could you improve?

Day 18: Launch again! Take what you've learned thus far and identify a few specific tweaks. Does the price need to change? Do you need more information on the sales page? Relaunch with your new offer.

Day 19: Just as retail stores frame the first dollar they receive, find a way to celebrate the beginning of your side hustle by commemorating the first check you cash, the email notification of your first customer, or something else. The point is to take joy in your success and, better yet, in knowing that the best is yet to come!

Note: Whether or not you do one of these each day doesn't matter much, but the general process does. Follow along and adapt as you build your own hustle.

HOW MUCH MONEY WILL YOUR PROJECT MAKE?

Wouldn't it be great if you knew exactly how much money your side hustle will bring in? Unless your sales or clients are capped somehow, a precise estimate may not be possible—and that's okay, because if business takes off, it's good to be pleasantly surprised.

However, you can probably make *some* kind of estimate. As you're evaluating different options and ideas, understanding the income potential for each one will help you make decisions.

In Chapter 4, you heard about Daniel Vlcek, the Czech immigrant who was surprised to learn he could make a decent living with only a small number of clients. This revelation was key, because before he began working on his own, he always imagined he'd need a ton of clients before he could "make it."

Here's how you can make your estimates.

Income Projection Tool

Example Project 1: Build a Better Mousetrap

This product-based project assumes that you've found a way to build or make something (in this case, a mousetrap) that has a fixed cost per unit.

> *Startup costs: $250*
>
> *Sales price per unit: $50*
>
> *Expenses per unit: $10*
>
> *Profit per unit: $40*
>
> *Sell one mousetrap a day = $40 profit*
>
> *Sell three mousetraps a day = $120 profit*
>
> *Maximum mousetraps per day = $300 (There is technically no limit to the number of units of a physical product you could sell. However, in many business ventures, you tend to encounter a natural "ceiling" after a bit of experimentation. If you aren't sure what it will be, estimate low.)*

Bottom line: If you sell one mousetrap a day, you'll earn an average profit of $1,200 a month. Every mousetrap after the first sale adds another $40 a day.

Example Project 2: Resumé Revisionist

This time-based project assumes that you have access to a regular supply of people who need the service you are offering. In this case, there is no fixed cost per unit, but the time commitment is especially important, since it's a limited resource.

Startup costs: $100

Sales price per service: $200

Time commitment per service: 90 minutes

Sell one resumé service a week: $200

Maximum resumé services per day = 1

Bottom line: If you sell one resumé revision service each week, you'll earn an average of $800 a month in exchange for six hours of work. Assuming 22 weekdays in an average month, the maximum you could earn in this scenario is $4,400 a month in exchange for 33 hours of work.

Of course, there are far more detailed methods of analysis if you need to be more precise. The point of this one is to *keep it simple*. Much of the time you just need a general idea of what's possible and what kind of investment is worth your time. The reality is that you don't usually know which projects will take off and which won't. This kind of exercise will show you which are worth trying.

It may sound obvious, but when choosing between different ideas you're equally attracted to, choose the idea with more income potential. In my case, I once faced a decision between making a set of branded posters and developing an online course. Both projects seemed interesting, but I didn't have time to do both. Once I ran an income analysis, the answer was clear: posters would be fun but had very limited earning potential. The online course would also be fun, but along with it came the possibility to make much more income. I chose the course.

THE 24-HOUR PRODUCT

After spending a few years working on a series of software projects, Idaho native Nathan Barry knew a few things about making products. He'd even written and published an entire book on the topic in just 60 days. But while he'd committed to working full-time on a project he hoped would exceed his earlier successes, he still had the itch to jump into a new thing every once in a while.

There was one idea in particular that had been on his mind for a long time, but he didn't want to divert his attention from the full-time gig. What to do? You may have guessed the answer from the headline: Nathan decided to create the complete product, a "10 Days to Better Design" guide, in just 24 hours.

He conducted the experiment in public, video-blogging updates every hour or so throughout the day. In the first couple of hours, he outlined the guide and brainstormed ideas for names with an eager audience of followers. By the time he went to bed, he had much of the guide written. The next day he was up at 5:15 a.m. and working hard on a basic website.

As promised, Nathan debuted the guide at the 24-hour

mark. He didn't quite finish *everything*, but he was close. More than 90 people bought the guide immediately, for a total profit of just over $1,000. A day and a half later, as more people caught up with the experiment, he had surpassed $3,000. Not bad for a day's work!

4½ QUESTIONS TO ANSWER WHEN MAKING YOUR OWN 24-HOUR PRODUCT

Call it your personal "hackathon," a type of event popular in tech circles where small teams compete to launch startups or solve a specific problem in a limited period of time, typically fueled by caffeine and the occasional break to play ping-pong. You too can use this model to make a quick-and-dirty product in a short period of time. All you need is 24 hours and, to be fair, a bit of advance preparation so you know what you're getting into.

The plan of attack isn't that different from the 19 Days to Hustle plan outlined on pages 161–164, just greatly accelerated. And if you're going to do it in a single day, you'll need to decide on a few things right away.

1. What is the product?

If you're going to make something in 24 hours, most likely it will be some sort of knowledge-based product. Consider what you know that can be taught through writing, audio, video, or some other format.

2. How will you sell it?

Keep it simple. Unless you have an easy way to ship something, distribute your 24-hour product online.

3. What's the price?

Pricing based on value is always good, but you probably shouldn't charge a fortune for something you create very quickly. Besides, for a quick product, you might as well try to get it into the hands of as many people as possible.

Oh, and there's one more big thing . . .

4. How will you get other people involved?

Nathan's 24-hour project was a success because he invited people to follow along and join him. In fact, he asked for their input, creating a publicly shared document where anyone could ask questions and even offer suggestions on the product's final name. This created a shared experience that was interesting for others and motivating for Nathan, especially when he received comments like "This is fun, and I'll buy whatever it is as soon as it's ready."

Bonus question: what are you waiting for?

THE "MO' MONEY" DAY
(A.K.A. HOW TO MAKE SMALL AMOUNTS OF
MONEY WHENEVER YOU WANT)

Here's a fun activity: once in a while, set aside a dedicated block of hours, typically the majority of a working day, to spend specifically on brainstorming things that can be done to improve or add to your current cash flow. I used to call this a personal finance day, but then I had a better idea: a block of tasks like this can essentially be a "Mo' Money" day—a day set aside to tidy up your work and finances, all for the purpose of *making mo' money*.

Here are a few things I typically work on during a Mo' Money day. Your tasks may vary, of course.

Sell your unused stuff. Recently I realized I had purchased a pair of shoes a while back but had never worn them. It was too late to return them, but I was able to sell them at a local used clothing store for $44.

Sure, you could argue that this was actually a loss, because I purchased them for more. That's true, but the point is that I wasn't using them. They were essentially valueless while sitting in my closet, but they turned into $44 during a five-minute errand.

Audit your credit or debit card statements. When I did this recently, I saw that my cell phone provider had overcharged me by more than $100 during a trip to Canada. I also noticed a duplicate charge from another vendor. I followed up and got these charges removed. It may have been my money to begin with, but if I hadn't done the audit, it would have just disappeared.

Cancel your unused services. Is there anything you're paying for but not using? Cancel it and get the equivalent of free money in your bank account every month. *Bam.*

You may also want to . . .

- Call your cable or cell phone provider to ask for a better deal

- Review the interest rates on any credit cards or investment accounts; then call the credit card company and try to negotiate them down
- Rebalance your investment portfolio (if you have one)
- Open a new savings account for an incentivized bonus
- Set financial goals, both long-term and short-term

What would you add to the list?

HOW DOES A SIDE HUSTLE FIT INTO THE WORK YOU WERE MEANT TO DO?

At this point you could be thinking, what does selling groceries have to do with finding the work you were meant to do? How does driving Uber passengers around or cleaning strangers' homes via an online service contribute to happiness? But remember the point: side hustles generate disproportionate amounts of satisfaction for relatively little investment of time or effort. They allow you to keep doing what you do best at your day job, while exploring other passions and ambitions during off-hours.

They also add some variety to your work life. Even if you're completely fulfilled and have found the work you were born to do in your day job, everyone likes to mix it up once in a while. Moreover, many side hustles turn into something bigger. Sometimes they provide the spark of motivation or inspiration for that career change you always wanted to make or that business you wanted to build. They can provide the financial safety net that enables you to take other risks or pursue a grand plan.

Even if not, it simply feels good to see extra money coming in from something you made. The bottom line is that a side hustle can be a low-risk, low-commitment way to test the waters for something bigger—and earn some extra money at the same time. There's no good reason not to try, and every good reason why it might turn out to have amazing upside.

Don't get hung up in indecision paralysis. Set your minimum wage and start panning for gold!

"I make a lot more money than I made in my old job, and likely more than I'd ever make if I'd stayed in the profession. It can be difficult to create your own income, but once you get over that hump, you have potential to make far more than you did before."

—ALEXIS, AGE 34, FOUNDER OF A CONTENT MARKETING COMPANY

8

You, Inc.

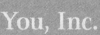

OBJECTIVE:

Build a Small Empire

Sometimes the job you want doesn't exist—and usually when that happens it's because you don't actually want a job, you want full control of your income and career. Many people who work for themselves believe this is actually the safest and most secure career path. This chapter is for those of you who want to quit working for someone else and take matters into your own hands—without going to business school and without getting into debt.

There's a classic business principle called "first-mover advantage." It means that when all other variables are equal, the company or organization that enters a market first will be the default leader. According to this theory, it's not necessarily *impossible* to topple a first mover, but the first mover will have a built-in head start.

First-mover advantage applies to plenty of big industries and markets, but when it comes to building a small to medium business (You, Inc.) it may actually be better to be second, third, or tenth to enter the market.[*]

Consider the well-known parable of the early worm. We're told that the early bird gets the worm, and perhaps that's true. But what if you're the worm? If you're the worm and you wake up and stick your neck out too early, you're sure to get eaten. If you're sticking your neck out into a new market or venture, far better to be the late worm. The early bird may get the worm, but the late worm gets to live.

HOW TO MAKE $101,971 SELLING T-SHIRTS

Benny Hsu struck gold when he was 37 years old, and he didn't do it by being an early worm. A former app designer who was curious about how to sell something to people he

---

[*] "Moving first is a tactic, not a goal. It's much better to be a last mover." —Peter Thiel

didn't know, Benny had a goal of entering an all-new line of work. He'd always been interested in fashion, and particularly in T-shirt designs. Earlier efforts at screen-printing a bunch of shirts had required a big initial investment, and he also had to be around to ship them out if orders came in. Now a new technology allowed him to create shirts with as few as ten orders, and without carrying any inventory at all.

There was just one problem: he had no customers. Having watched other people use online ads to target people based on specific demographics and occupations, he decided to try growing his customer base through targeted advertising. Twenty-one times he tried to sell his T-shirt designs to targeted users on Facebook, with a goal of recouping his advertising costs and making a reasonable profit—and 21 times he failed to make a single sale.

Still, the failures weren't costly; he spent a maximum of just $10 on each experiment, and each time he kept detailed notes on what went wrong. Finally, on the 22nd attempt, he found a winner: before he'd reached the $10 cap, he finally had his first sale. This time he let the ad campaign run its course. At the end, he'd spent $81.72 and earned $112.25, for a profit of $30.53.

FAILED EXPERIMENTS (#1–21)	SUCCESSFUL EXPERIMENT (#22)
$10 × 21 = $210 (a.k.a. startup cost)	Revenue ($112.25) – Ad cost ($81.72) = Profit ($30.53)

Thirty bucks wasn't enough to put Benny on the path to riches, but he was encouraged by the success. He knew that the failed experiments had been heading in the right direction all along, so he kept optimizing and fine-tuning with every campaign. Every morning he'd wake up and immediately check his numbers to see what had happened overnight. Every night he'd upload new ads in anticipation of another day's tests. He had more successes, and more failures, too—but he'd quickly drop the failures and keep rolling with the winners.

Just one month in, he'd made up for the failed campaigns and broken even, having spent and made nearly $1,000. After that, it was smooth sailing.

Five months in, he'd spent more than $50,000 on ads . . . but he'd *made* more than $150,000. That's when he realized this wasn't just a side hustle; this was a full-time gig. Benny's "experiment" has now been running for more than two years, and he continues to design T-shirts full-time. "The freedom this business has brought me is incredible," he told me. "I can work on something fun, do it from anywhere, and make money while I sleep."

Benny wasn't the first person to ever sell T-shirts, and plenty of other people were experimenting with Facebook ads. He wasn't the early bird, in other words—but by continually refining the process through a series of careful tests, he was able to create a reliable, high-earning business.

SELF-EMPLOYMENT IS THE NEW PENSION

In *The $100 Startup*, I outlined the model that thousands of independent entrepreneurs have used to create money-making ventures, typically without any formal business training. In short, this model is:

1. Do what you love, sort of. I say "sort of" because you can't just do *anything* you want and expect to make money, but there's probably *something* you can do that will accomplish that goal.

2. Find convergence between what you value and what other people will pay for. Benny believed there was a market for handmade T-shirts, because he and many of his friends liked to wear shirts with unique designs. To prove his theory, he put it to the test in a real-world marketplace.

3. Start quickly and with a low level of investment. Once Benny was able to print T-shirts on demand, his startup costs were negligible—just $10 for each of the 21 failed ads.

4. See what happens and change course if needed as you go along. Benny used Facebook as a giant testing lab for his designs, and adapted them according to what his customers wanted.

This model can be used whether or not you've ever started a business before, and whether or not you have any desire to go full-time in the world of independent work. In the last chapter you learned how to launch a successful side hustle; here you'll learn how to grow a side hustle or other part-time project into something more serious.

In Chapter 7, you also learned how to make a rough estimate of a side hustle's profit potential (it's back on pages 165–166 if you want a refresher). When you have a project that's going well and it seems like it could take off to new heights if you devoted more time to it, that's when you want to get serious about ramping it up into a full-fledged business. But how?

Growing a side hustle into a business is actually a lot simpler than it sounds. With any product or service, there are only two ways to grow:

1. Sell more to existing customers
2. Sell to more customers

It really is that simple, and the kind of business you have may dictate what strategy is best. For example, with Benny's T-shirt business, he's probably not going to get rich selling shirts to the same customers over and over. It's nice when people buy more than one shirt (since he doesn't have to pay for advertising for any repeat buyers), but most people don't need a whole new wardrobe of T-shirts every month. In his case, growth depends on reaching more people.

In many other businesses, however, it's much easier to sell more to existing customers. The best way to do this is by developing additional products or extensions of the existing services. Your existing customers will likely jump at your new offerings, and any *new* customers that come along for the ride are essentially a bonus.

BE YOUR OWN VENTURE CAPITAL

If you don't invest in yourself, who will? Heath Padgett, a young videographer and jack-of-many-trades from Austin, Texas, originally wanted to build up a safety net before leaving his job at a startup. But as he tried to grow a project during his off-hours, he realized that this plan wouldn't work.

"Starting a business on nights and weekends might be good for some people," he said, "but I didn't have enough pressure to go all in with my own projects. I had a nice, comfy job supporting me, so if I didn't work on my business that day I was still being paid. I knew that if I wanted to be successful and really give myself a chance, I would have to jump in headfirst. If I crashed, I would crash hard. I also realized that we look like a fool only if we fail. If we win, people celebrate and think we're really smart. I embraced this mentality to begin my journey."

Heath adopted a strategy of increasing his value and worth in every aspect of his life. He continued to develop his skills by learning new technology and studying what other videographers were doing. He made connections, like finding a debut author who had written a compelling book about embracing risk but needed help making a marketing trailer. He took risks and experimented, driving around the country in an RV with his wife, Alyssa, working odd jobs in different states and chronicling their adventures.

All along the way, he also invested in himself by taking advantage of every opportunity that arose. The stakes weren't terribly high, after all—if it didn't work out, he could always go back to a traditional job. Heath chose to take the leap and see what developed along the way.

If you decide you're ready to be an investor in You, Inc., there are four areas you need to consider.

> 1. *Skills.* Improve both the technical aspects of your work (just as Heath set out to learn about the new technology in videography) and your soft skills such as writing, reading, negotiating, and more (see Chapter 4 for more advice on this).
> 2. *Connections.* Commit to networking and meeting everyone you can (like the debut author who gave Heath his first gig).
> 3. *Experiments.* Try new things and expose yourself to new places, people, and ideas (as Heath did on his year-long cross-country tour).
> 4. *Opportunities.* Say yes to business deals and opportunities (Heath said yes to almost every opportunity, even if they weren't 100 percent related to what he eventually wanted to do).

As you go along, remember to pay attention to your inbox—or however you hear from customers, clients, and

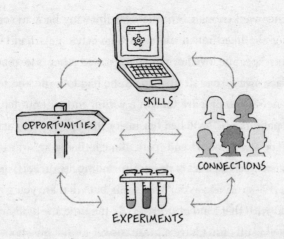

partners—because you may find more answers and ideas there to help you take your side hustle to the next level.

THE PASSION PLANNER

Can a college student have a midlife crisis? Maybe not, but Angelia Trinidad did have an experience in her sophomore year that caused her to rethink everything. Angelia was raised in a strict Asian American household, the kind where getting a B meant she'd somehow failed, so she had high expectations to meet in her UCLA pre-med studies. So far, so good—but she wasn't happy.

Fortunately, she'd mastered the game of studying hard, memorizing reams of molecular chemistry information, and testing well, so good grades came fairly easily. This may have pleased her hard-driving parents, but she knew medicine wasn't her dream career. Even though she liked science well enough, Angelia kept thinking back to something she liked much more. In high school, art had been her escape. She loved drawing and called it her "safe place," a place away from all the papers she had to write and tests she needed to prepare for. On a whim, and without telling her parents, she switched her major from pre-med to art.

The story doesn't end there, though. Being an art major came with challenges of its own, including the dreaded question that everyone asks: "That's fun, but what are you going to do with that kind of degree?" By the time she graduated, Angelia still didn't have a great answer to that question. Instead of feeling inspired, she felt stuck and scared, knowing that she was no longer going into medicine and wasn't sure what she should do instead. She was a classic overachiever who suddenly found herself with no more tests to take or art projects to throw herself into. What's more, even though she was happy to have the art degree, she didn't actually want to be a capital-A Artist. It just wasn't the work she was born to do, she realized. So what was?

Angelia found part of the answer by looking not just to her skills (the ability to study hard, test well, and organize her life) or simply to her passions (art), but rather by looking to the intersection between the two. By combining her love for the drawing she used to do as well as her knack for creative thinking and ability to prepare well for a busy schedule of tests, papers, and extracurricular activities, she came up with the idea to create a prototype for a new kind of day planner, a printed journal that would help students and non-students alike keep up with all their activities while also prompting them to be creative and have fun. She called it the Passion Planner, and it was unlike any time management tool she'd seen before (and as an organized person always looking for an edge, she'd seen a lot of them).

It certainly wasn't medicine, and it wasn't quite art, either. It was a unique marriage of something that combined Angelia's different passions, interests, and skills—and it was a huge hit. The validation that it was also something she could get *paid* for came when she first offered it to the public in a Kickstarter campaign, which raised more than $48,000 on an initial goal of $19,000. Then she did it again a few months later, raising more than $100,000 for a different, slimmer version.

But wait, there's more: a third Kickstarter campaign went completely viral, buoyed by rave reviews from everyone who'd purchased an earlier version. When the final countdown ended, Angelia and her growing team gathered around a laptop and refreshed the screen one more time. The results were incredible: 23,626 backers pledged $658,434 to help bring this project to life.

By this point, it wasn't just the huge number of backers (which were essentially customers in this context) that was so exciting. Soon Angelia and company were donating planners to schools, libraries, and organizations. Then Electronic Arts, the gaming company, placed a bulk order for all its employees. The Passion Planner was suddenly no longer just a passion project—it had become a real business.

THE ZERO-TO-ONE TEST

Peter Thiel, the venture capitalist and founder of PayPal, proposed a model for understanding the key to massive business growth, especially among technology companies. He calls this "Zero-to-One," and distinguishes a Zero-to-One business from other kinds of businesses: "Horizontal progress means copying things that work—going from 1 to n. It's easy to imagine because we already know what it looks like. Vertical progress means doing new things—going from 0 to 1. It's harder to imagine because it requires doing something that nobody else has ever done. If you take one typewriter and build 100, you have made horizontal progress. If you have a typewriter and build a word processor, you have made vertical progress."

This illustration may be helpful in understanding the difference:

Most people who read this book aren't setting out to build a massive technology business (although perhaps some of you will). Even so, the Zero-to-One test is interesting to consider when you are deciding whether to move from side hustle to all-in entrepreneur.

Lots of side hustles are essentially 1-to-n projects, and that's fine. Being useful and helpful will never go out of style. But if you have the chance to go from 0 to 1, creating something truly new and different, you might want to grow out of side hustle mode and prepare for something much bigger.

As scary as going out on your own can be, try to resist the temptation to trade one semi-secure situation for another by copying an existing idea or simply joining up with an existing business. Instead, create your own security by going Zero-to-One and building your own small (or not so small) empire from the ground up.

WHEN TO QUIT YOUR JOB, AND WHEN TO TURN A SIDE HUSTLE INTO A FULL-TIME BUSINESS

Once you've decided to go all in, how do you know when the time is right? Unfortunately, there's no one-size-fits-all answer to this question. I've seen people quit jobs to devote themselves to their own ventures at many different stages. For Heath Padgett, the young videographer, and perhaps for others like him, starting on the side while holding down a day job *doesn't* work well. You may not have the time or bandwidth to grow the business while working another job full-time. But others prefer the safety net of having a reliable stream of income while scaling up their side project, even if it means sleeping less and working on their business nights and weekends.

There's one surefire way to make a decision if you're on the fence: *you quit your job when your business is making you enough money to live on*—not when it's merely promising and has potential, but when it's actually providing enough income to pay your bills, even if it's less than what you make in the job. Until then, resist the urge to quit unless you feel absolutely confident that your budding empire is on track for greater things.

A SHORT (YET COMPREHENSIVE) GUIDE TO THE TECHNOLOGY YOU NEED

People tend to assume that starting a successful company requires a ton of skills or experience with technology. But these days that couldn't be further from the case. Now, with tools like WordPress and Squarespace, anyone can build a website, market a product online, build a social media following, and so on—even if you've never written a line of code in your life.

As mentioned in Chapter 4, those who are comfortable using new technology will generally be more competitive in the new economy. This doesn't mean, however, that you need to geek out, become a coder, or rush out to buy the latest gadget every month. Remember that the whole point of going into business on your own is so you don't have to be a slave to anyone else, and in this case "anyone else" also includes technology. You don't need to master every innovation that comes around; you just need to use technology to accomplish your goals.

Here are some quick-and-dirty tips for developing the baseline technological skills you'll need to run your successful mini-empire.

- *Don't stress about the fact that social media is constantly changing.* There's a new network every day, so how do you keep up? Answer: you don't. Instead of trying to be *everywhere*, do a good job staying present and engaged with your fans on a couple of networks, and leave it at that.

- *Keep up with the main forms of communication.* Communication technology changes more slowly than social media, and here it's important to keep up. If you're emailing when everyone else is texting, or using an AOL email address while everyone else is on Gmail, you'll feel left behind.

- *Make sure you have a way to get paid.* I've mentioned this elsewhere in the book, but it bears repeating here: you can't make money if you don't have a way to get paid. Luckily, new technologies have made getting paid easier than ever. You can accept money for your goods or services just by setting up a free account with PayPal, Square, or several other systems. The most important thing to remember is to make it as easy as possible for the person who's sending you money. I once knew someone who hated PayPal and regularly turned away business by refusing to accept it. Here's a crazy idea: it doesn't matter what *you* think about any particular payment method but rather what your customers prefer.

- *You need some kind of website.* Like it or not, if Google can't find you, neither can your potential clients or customers. The good news is that you can set up a website or blog *in one hour or less* using WordPress, free software that is available for any computer. Pick up a free guide on how it works in the online resources section at BornforThisBook .com.

The point is, it's not that hard to set up an online business, even for the non-tech-savvy. And by the way, most of what you need to know, you can easily learn from the Internet. Google it and keep up!

THE THREE-MINUTE MBA

There are a number of misconceptions about business school, the biggest of which is that earning an MBA will help you learn how to start a business. If you want to be a middle manager in a big corporation, an MBA can be a good choice. The letters stand for "master of business administration," because what you learn is how to run someone else's business. If that's the work you were born to do, or if having those letters on your resumé will help you gain an automatic promotion or increased salary, an MBA may be a good investment. But for everyone else, and especially if you want to start and run a business of your own, it may be a lot better to stay out of school.

If you're not sure whether business school might be for you, this cheat sheet compares what you'll learn in business school to what you need to know to work for yourself. Notice how different these areas are.

Management

What you'll learn in business school:

- Case studies of how executives manage hundreds or thousands of employees working under them

What you need to know:

- How to work with all kinds of people and how to negotiate to get what you want

Operations

What you'll learn in business school:

- How to manage factories, hospitals, fleets of aircraft, oil and gas production facilities, and similar large-scale enterprises

What you need to know:

- How to manage the thing that makes you money

Finance

What you'll learn in business school:

- Stock and bond valuation models, forecasting and project evaluation, how to generate short-term profits to raise share prices

What you need to know:

- How to make enough money—whatever "enough" means to you—on a recurring basis

Accounting

What you'll learn in business school:

- How to prepare corporate financial statements, the amortization and depreciation of intangible assets, and more

What you need to know:

- How to pay the bills and keep up with the money you've made

Marketing

What you'll learn in business school:

- How to spend millions of dollars of other people's money on ad campaigns

What you need to know:

- How to reach people who want to buy your product, service, or offer

Statistics

What you'll learn in business school:

- Differential calculus, linear programming, something called "derivatives," and something about "frequency distribution"

What you need to know:

- Not much

Bonus: If you're still on the fence, be sure to check out Josh Kaufman's classic treatise *The Personal MBA*. It has a retail price of less than $20, so you'll save approximately $59,980 on tuition from a typical top-10 program.

If the time is right and you feel the urge, consider going all in on the business of you. Just remember to keep the Joy-Money-Flow model at the center of your considerations. If one of these key elements is missing, you'll have a much harder time building your own small (or not so small) empire. When you *do* find the right fit, your leap to freedom will land on solid ground. Don't join up with an entity that someone else owns and operates for their benefit—create your own security instead.

"I never had a eureka moment. I had a process of discovery that led me to something that paid well and provided the autonomy I craved."

—KELLY, AGE 35,
ONLINE COMMUNITY MANAGER

9

How to Become a Firefighter (or Whatever You Want)

OBJECTIVE:

Play the Game That Will Increase Your Odds

Stop playing the numbers game and never send out another resumé. Instead of betting the odds, play the game that improves your odds.

It's very hard to become a professional firefighter. With an average acceptance rate of less than 1 percent, many fire departments are actually more competitive than Stanford or Harvard. Each time openings are announced in a typical department, hundreds or even thousands of people take the test, and only a few pass. To become a firefighter, you have to be certified in first aid, truck driving, elevator operation, and more. It's also a physically demanding job, requiring heavy lifting in extreme conditions. Basically, you have to be very smart *and* very strong, and then you have to acquire a lot of specific knowledge that is used to save lives. The result is the classic conundrum for any highly skilled job: many are called, few are chosen. Or put more simply, becoming a professional firefighter isn't just hard. It's really, *really* hard. But not impossible.

At age 20, Shelli Rae Varela was a self-described bohemian artist living in Ontario, Canada. She had an aptitude for mechanical things, having grown up helping her dad fix trucks. But she also had a creative side, learning to draw at an early age and taking photos as soon as she could use a camera. One more thing: Shelli was five feet two inches tall and weighed 108 pounds. Her childhood nickname was "Peanut." From the outside, she looked like the very last person you'd ever expect to become a firefighter.

As a young adult she had spent a lot of time with a family friend who was going through a rough patch. The friend, Steve, was a firefighter in Toronto, and Shelli was enthralled with his stories of rescues and close calls. During his days away from the station, she'd go over to his house to talk. Once he ran out of stories, he started teaching her about the job itself.

One day they were in a car driving somewhere and Shelli spotted a truck with a Hazardous Materials label. Recalling the things Steve had taught her, she immediately pointed out that the label was incorrectly applied.

Steve was impressed. "Why don't you just apply for a job at the firehouse?" he asked.

At the time, female firefighters in Canada were few and far between. Furthermore, "Peanut" Varela didn't exactly have the physical appearance of a strong person of any gender. All the odds were against her, but the idea resonated right away.

That's what I want to do, she thought. *I'm going to become a firefighter.*

Becoming a firefighter requires many, many steps. Of the small number of people who manage to pass the written test, many fail the physical, get turned down in the interview because they're not a good fit, or otherwise just give up. To succeed and get hired, you have to make studying and preparing your full-time job for months, if not years.

Shelli had always been a go-getter. If she wanted something, she made it happen. Firefighting, though, wasn't so simple. She registered for the test in Toronto, then showed up to see 5,000 other people waiting at the convention hall. What were all these people doing there? *Oh,* she realized, *they all want to be firefighters.*

This exam, known in Canada as the National Fire Select Test, isn't something you can cram for the night before. Shelli had counted on her mechanical aptitude and all those lessons from Steve to get her through, but she hadn't realized how much more there was to learn. Needless to say, her first test results were subpar.

Still, she could retake the test an unlimited number of times, and she was willing to do whatever it took to improve her score. Over the next few months, she reverse-engineered the process of professional firefighting. She researched all of the skills that were required and set out to gain aptitude in each. Before too long, a pile of certificates accumulated in the folder that she always carried with her. She supported herself by working in a nail salon, but the focus was always that dream: *That's what I want to do. I'm going to become a firefighter.*

It took more than three years (or 1,162 days, to be precise) to turn this dream into reality. She knows the specific number because once she had that aha moment at age 20, she never stopped thinking about it. Every day, as she worked on various requirements or studied for another test, she visualized the phone call she'd receive when she was finally selected. Thinking of that call kept her motivated and focused on her studies.

She took the test eight more times, all over the province. Most of the time she passed, but with a lower score than the few people who made it to the next round. On one occasion she scored 92.5 percent—just shy of the 93 percent required to move on. So close! But each time her score got better and better.

Finally she earned the score required to move to the final stages of selection. Yet she still had hurdles to overcome. For one, the supervisors were skeptical of her physical abilities (remember, very few women had done this at the time, and Shelli was tiny), but she proved them wrong by exceeding the required results in the fitness exam.

And then one day the call came. She'd passed every-thing with flying colors, and the Mississauga Fire Depart-ment, Canada's sixth largest, offered her a job.

It turned out to be just what she had always dreamed of. She took the job, started the official training the following week, and never looked back. Despite all the odds stacked against her—the stiff competition, the grueling application process, her diminutive size—she succeeded. When I spoke with her, she had just finished her 21st year as a profes-sional firefighter.

HOW CAN YOU LAND *YOUR* DREAM JOB?

Let's get a depressing fact out of the way. Most advice about getting the job of your dreams is highly misleading and even damaging. As I was researching this chapter, I thought it would be good to see what the experts suggest as the best approach to getting a long-shot job—and what I found was either wrong, uninspiring, or both.

Writing in the *New York Times*, popular columnist Thomas Friedman advised graduates to "stand out." Em-ployers these days don't care where you went to school, he said, quoting from a Harvard education expert and a startup founder who had gone to Yale. The startup founder had worked for McKinsey, the multinational consulting group, and her partner had worked for Goldman Sachs.

That's great. All you need to do is go to an Ivy
League school—presumably someone else will
pick up the $40,000 a year tab?—and then get
a highly selective and well-paid position. After
that, you'll be able to "stand out."

Most of the experts, it seems, treat getting a job as a
pure numbers game. The more jobs you apply for, they
say, the greater your odds of landing one. But in reality
it doesn't work that way, at least not directly. Why not?
One reason is that the application process, especially for
entry-level and mid-level positions, has experienced a
serious case of application inflation in recent years. As
the job market has gotten more and more competitive,
applicants—not just new graduates but job seekers of all
ages—typically panic and send out as many resumés as
they can, all in hopes of a single interview. This mass application strategy rarely works, though, because research
shows that most people are hired outside the normal application process.

The bigger problem is that the logic behind the "throw
spaghetti at the wall and see what sticks" approach is fundamentally flawed. Think about it. If every job applicant
is sending out, say, 75 additional resumés, that means that
employers are receiving, at a very minimum, 75 additional
applications for every available job. It's a problem that's
been growing ever since the late 1990s, when online job
listings became common and applicants no longer had to
pick up a printed newspaper (remember those?) to pore

over the classified ads. Your college career office may have continued to maintain a number of thick three-ring binders with job info from local businesses, but most students went straight to the computer and logged in to search.

In some ways, the online job listings made things easier for job seekers. You could now search anywhere for any kind of job, and often apply right there on the website, no printing or mailing out of resumés required. But in other ways, the easily accessible listings and instant application process have actually made things *worse* by increasing the sheer number of applicants for every job. It sounds crazy until you realize that it doesn't require much work to apply for most jobs. If all you need to do is click a button to throw your name in the hat, there's nothing to stop anyone from simply clicking buttons over and over.

There are two ways to adapt in this environment: try to be better and work harder than everyone else (send out 76 resumés instead of 75—keep clicking the application button!), or approach the problem from an entirely different angle. Chances are you probably can't become a better button clicker than everyone else. Besides, didn't that expensive higher education teach you something better than clicking buttons?

STOP PLAYING THE NUMBERS GAME

If you want to approach the problem from a different angle, you have to stop playing the numbers game and start playing a game that actually improves your odds. Let's go back to the casino we stopped in briefly way back in Chapter 3. Most people who visit the casino are gamblers, meaning that they are essentially giving away their money to the house over time. Sure, the house will keep their drinks topped off, and maybe they'll even get a free buffet in exchange for their donation, but over time, most people who play casino games will lose.

There are exceptions, though. In Atlantic City, I met a guy I'll call Dan who works as a professional video poker player. He's a real person, not a composite, but he asked me not to use his real name. Over the past two years, he's been working on a strategy that gives him a tiny but profitable 0.02 percent edge.

The strategy, in brief, is to *choose the right machine*. All gaming machines are calibrated in a certain way to provide more or less winnings to the casino. Dan figured out an optimal strategy of machine selection, which when combined with near-perfect play (a skill that actually isn't that hard to acquire, since you always make the same decisions once you know what to do) resulted in him making an average of $200 for every eight-hour shift he put in at Atlantic City.

If we apply Dan's winning strategy to your job search, the key action isn't to apply for more and more jobs. The key is to apply for the *right* jobs. How do you pick the "machine" that will give you the best odds?

SMART GAMBLING: STEPS 1–5

As with most things in life, when trying to find and land your dream job, it's helpful to consider the other party's perspective. Do companies want to wade through thousands of resumés for a single position? Not really. When filling positions in the workplace, successful companies and organizations just want to find the best possible people, in the least amount of time.

In other words, your goals and theirs are somewhat aligned.

When it comes time to get a job, most people follow a well-trodden path. They do things like:

- Go to a job fair or recruitment session

- Browse job posting websites

- Polish their resumé or CV

- Check in with industry and alumni networks

- Update their LinkedIn profile

These kinds of activities are very good at helping you think you're making progress when you may just be running in circles. Why? Think about how many other smart, qualified applicants are currently doing the exact same things. These activities might feel productive, but they probably won't help you find your dream job. In a highly competitive environment, just keeping pace with what others are doing isn't enough. You need to be doing something to give yourself a real advantage.

Here are a few steps that will actually help you improve your odds.

1. Decide on the job title you want. If you want to land the job posted as "human resources manager," that's what you'll get—well, at least if you're the lucky person to make it through all those rounds of resumé filtering. But what if you created your own title and decided to find a company or organization that was willing to make room for it? Suddenly your competition just got much smaller.

In talking with people who'd been creative with a self-styled job title, I heard from a "chief happiness officer," a role that has now been filled at several startups but actually dates back to 2003, when McDonald's delegated happiness duties to the Ronald McDonald clown character. I also heard from "Mayor" Tony Bacigalupo, who runs a co-working space in New York City.

If you could have any job title in the world, what would yours look like?

2. Create an artist's statement that describes your future self. Instead of the standard resumé, many painters, sculptors, and other visual artists typically create an "artist's statement" that describes their work and purpose. It's easy to see the difference between a strong artist's statement and a weak one. The weak one contains a lot of big words, uses passive instead of active language, and goes on forever.[*] Stronger artists' statements get to the point quickly and leave little room for confusion:

- My watercolor paintings are about nostalgia and sentimentality.

- I create sculptures and other physical installations to show the evolution of humankind and its impact on the environment.

- My weekly podcast explores how the world of work is changing, especially for baby boomers and others who are more accustomed to traditional careers.

Naturally, most artists' statements are composed for creative endeavors, not job applications, but why not modify the concept for something more career-oriented? The key is to focus half on your past accomplishments and half on what you hope to achieve in the future. Short is good, but it's not a race to find the fewest possible words. Here are a few examples:

- As a successful middle-school teacher, I developed strong skills in communication and leadership. My

---

[*] Unfortunately, weak artists' statements are all too common. For examples of particularly ridiculous ones, visit artybollocks.com.

goal is to apply these skills in a new career in public relations.

· Using my proven skills and five years of experience as a front-end developer, I want to help an
organization make tremendous improvements in
its systems and networks.

· I graduated with a 3.9 GPA (unfortunately I got
one A–, in high-level calculus). I'm ready to help
companies improve profitability and develop new
sources of income.

3. Ask five people for help. Send out a series of personal emails asking for specific help. Don't send emails to
everyone in your network, and don't use BCC—most people will just delete those messages. And don't put out an
impersonal post on Facebook or send out a generic tweet.
The key is to get as specific as possible about how these
people can uniquely help. Ask for leads on getting the kind
of job you want, or even just an introduction to someone
who might be able to steer you in the right direction. See
what happens. Then ask five other people.

When you get an introduction to an influential person,
see if you can meet with him or her, even for a brief period of time. This won't always be possible, but when it is,
strive to make a good impression and listen more than you
talk. Unless the other person clearly wants to keep going,
end the meeting when the requested amount of time is up.
Afterward, send a quick follow-up thanking the other per-

son for his or her time. If appropriate, make one specific request for a further connection, opportunity, or interview.

4. Use "demonstrated interest" as a strategy for life, not just college applications. As colleges continue to be deluged with applications, they've started weighing a new factor in addition to test scores and GPAs. In short, they want to know if applicants *really* care about the school they're applying to, or if it's just one of many in a big batch of applications. This factor, which admissions officers refer to as "demonstrated interest," can be hard to quantify, but it refers to things like:

- Has the applicant visited the school for an official tour?

- Why does the applicant feel that this school in particular is a good fit?

- How will this applicant make a positive contribution to our culture?

Just as successful college applicants are now doing everything they can to show demonstrated interest to the schools they're most interested in, so you can apply a similar strategy to job searches. For example, when Shelli Rae Varela chose to become a firefighter, she went out and learned everything she could about what the job entailed. Whenever she encountered a skill or area of knowledge that was unfamiliar, she eagerly asked questions, read books, or even took courses to ensure she was fully qualified. She really, *really* wanted to become a firefighter, and she showed it.

I began working with my assistant, Ashley, when she emailed me out of the blue and offered to help with anything I needed. We'd met briefly a couple of months before, and she'd struck me as hardworking and trustworthy. At the time I was struggling with a really boring task: I had a huge Microsoft Excel spreadsheet with thousands of lines of address data that had to be organized. I knew the task would take at least several hours, if not longer. I almost apologized when I offered it to her: "Uh, how would you like to spend up to eight hours staring at an Excel spreadsheet?"

Her response surprised me. "That would be great!" she said.

Not only did she enthusiastically agree to complete the task, she even spent extra time reading up about spreadsheets and watching training videos on YouTube. It was demonstrated interest if I ever saw it, and a few months and a few more trial tasks later, I offered her a full-time job—and felt fortunate when she accepted.

5. Decide to just start working and see what happens. Don't have time for all that pesky application paperwork? Maybe you should just show up somewhere and start working. This has actually been done!

Mark Suster was working as a consultant in London when he heard about a new company project that was kicking off in Tokyo. Mark had grown up with a love of Asian culture and had always wanted to work in Japan, but he knew the odds of being randomly assigned to the project were slim. He also knew if he requested the assignment and was then turned down—a likely scenario, given that his skills were needed elsewhere—he couldn't just disobey orders and head to Tokyo.

So he split the difference: he didn't ask for the assignment, he simply "self-accepted" it. After purchasing a plane ticket (one that he wasn't sure would be reimbursable), he flew to Tokyo over the weekend and showed up at the local office on Monday morning. "What are you doing here?" the project manager asked.

"I heard you needed help," he said—though, by his own admission, part of the conversation may have been lost in translation.

The company gave him something to do for the week—he was already there, after all, so why not?—and he did it extremely well. At the end of the week, they asked him to come back again the following Monday. Mark ended up staying for six months. Before he left Japan, the lead partner asked him to consider a permanent transfer to the local office. He was ready to move on to something else by that point, but the risky gamble had paid off.

CHOOSE THE SLOT MACHINE WITH THE SHORTEST LINE

What if your problem isn't necessarily *finding* or *getting* a job, but rather advancing to the level or position you want? It's not always possible to self-accept a promotion or skip steps on a corporate ladder. Consider a typical military career, for example, which advances officers and enlisted soldiers according to a rigid, linear schedule with few opportunities for skipping steps. For someone coming in on the bottom rung of the ladder, a rough outline of the first 20 years of service looks like this:

> Private (E-2): the first 6 months
> Private First Class (E-3): at 1 year
> Specialist/Corporal (E-4): at 18 months
> Sergeant (E-5): at 4.2 years
> Staff Sergeant (E-6): at 8.5 years
> Sergeant First Class (E-7): at 13.6 years
> Master Sergeant/First Sergeant (E-8): at 17 years
> Sergeant Major (E-9): at 20.8 years
>
> *Source: U.S. Army Recruitment Guide, 2015.*

Of course, there's some variance to this schedule. Some fields promote faster than others, and some branches of service promote earlier. And after you climb the initial rungs, further promotions are supposed to be based entirely on merit. Generally speaking, though, this is the approximate timeline. You can usually predict with a good deal of certainty how far you'll advance based on your age when you enter service and how long you stay in.

Let's say you're thinking of joining the military but don't feel a specific calling to any particular branch of service. All things being equal, why not join the branch that promotes faster? In other words, if you were standing in front of five slot machines with lines of varying lengths and they all had the same odds of success, the best choice would be the one with the shortest line.

Many companies are like this, too. When you have a choice between a role that offers limited, linear advancement potential and one that could bring greater reward much sooner, you might as well take a hard look at the more accelerated option. If you're qualified for more than one field, and each is attractive, why not enter the field that provides quicker advancement?

HOW TO GET A BOOK DEAL, AND HOW "WEAK TIES" CAN HELP YOU MORE THAN CLOSE FRIENDS

Even if you've been living in your basement, subsisting on ramen and rarely emerging into the sunlight, chances are you already know a lot of people who can help with your career goals. By deliberately cultivating these relationships—in a natural, non-creepy way—you can rely on them when you're looking for a job, building a business, or even seeking personal advice or support.

There's a popular principle from sociology called "the strength of weak ties." The short version of this principle is that *our acquaintances can open more doors to more people, and thus introduce us to more opportunities, than our friends can.* This is because we tend to travel in the same circles as our friends, but people we know only casually ("weak ties") tend to have much different networks of friends and other acquaintances. It's been well documented that for this reason, weak ties are incredibly valuable when it comes to looking for a job. But even more important than having a lot of weak ties is having the *right* weak ties.

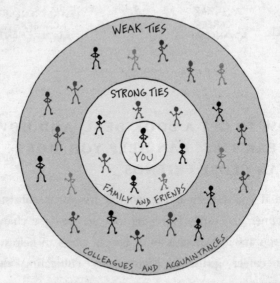

Here's a real-world example of this principle in action. When I first wanted to write a book, I didn't know a lot of other authors I could lean on for advice. I dutifully searched online and went to the library to research books on the process of connecting with an agent or publisher. I then set out to contact editors and agents myself, but I didn't get very far (most people simply didn't reply to my queries).

When that approach didn't work, I started asking everyone I knew if they had any advice or connections they could pass on. I finally connected with a guy who would soon become my literary agent, David Fugate, through a referral from one of his other authors who had been reading my blog, unbeknownst to me. Seven years later, David and I have worked together on four books. I've also been able to refer several other successful authors to him. In a way, meeting David was the human equivalent of Dan's winning casino game. It's a very strong relationship that was initially forged from a weak tie.

The example is relevant for much more than writing books. It relates to the principle at the heart of this chapter. Success isn't found completely in persistence; it's found in working hard *and* smart. Try, try again, sure—but try again in a strategic manner. The point is that just as with applying to jobs, when it comes to building relationships, quality matters over quantity.

The goal, in other words, is not necessarily to connect with more people, but to connect with *more of the right kinds of people.*

SOCIAL MEDIA IN REAL LIFE: A LESSON FROM GRANDMA UNA

Whether you're hunting for a job, moving up in your career, or building a new venture, people are always advising you to "use social media." But how? These days, telling people to "use social media" is like saying "use your words." What else would you use to communicate?

Social networks are funny things. Nearly every week you hear of a new one that's cropped up, and it can all be a little confusing. Should you set up a hundred profiles on a hundred networks, then spend all your time posting updates? Should you hire a virtual assistant who pretends to be you on Twitter? You probably already know that neither of these ideas is good. What matters is figuring out who *your* people are and where they hang out. That's where you should be, not necessarily on the hottest new network, and certainly not spread so thin that you don't have time to actually do the real work you're trying to become known for.

No matter which network or platform or tool you use to reach people, the most important goal is to be authentic and genuine. I used to joke that when I first started blogging, I had only five readers, and Grandma Una was one of them. Then I discovered that she'd signed up for my newsletter with two unique email addresses, so Grandma represented a full 40 percent of the audience.

Another family joke began when she started receiving the newsletter I sent. At first she didn't realize that it was a group mailing—she thought I was writing only to her. "Chris wrote me a nice long note the other day," she'd tell my parents when they visited. My dad tried to explain that the newsletter was actually being sent to a bunch of people all at once, but the next time he'd stop by, she'd say the same thing: "I got another nice note from Chris in my email."

We all laughed about this for a while, but the next time I sat down to write my newsletter, I remembered the story and its underlying lesson. A good writer doesn't actually write for the masses, even if the masses eventually end up reading. A good writer seeks to build connection with the reader, and it starts with considering that person on the other side of the screen or page.

Maybe my grandma was right: essentially, I was writing only to her. She had signed up on my website. When the email appeared in her inbox, it was something she'd asked for. The next step was up to me: would I deliver something that was valuable, or at least interesting? That's when I vowed to try to always write like I was writing only to my grandma or someone else I cared about—a policy that has served me well ever since.

You don't have to be a professional writer to follow this advice. Even without a newsletter or blog, you can still strive to maintain the same level of authenticity in your social media relationships, no matter what you do—or aspire to do—for your career or job.[*]

---

[*] Thankfully, she hasn't unsubscribed yet. Grandma, if you're reading this, the emails go only to you.

HOW TO WIN THE FINAL HAND

Questions to Ask on a Job Interview

So you finally landed that big, long-shot interview. How can you continue to beat the odds stacked against you and get the job offer? Much interview advice is basic and boring, but there's something that career experts agree on: it's important to come prepared with some questions of your own. This is as much to satisfy your own informational needs as it is to look curious and smart. After all, you're not just looking to serve as a cog in someone else's machine; you want to be sure the job will offer your perfect balance of joy, money, and flow.

Here are a few questions to ask (in your own words):

- What's the greatest problem your team is currently experiencing?

- What's the most valuable contribution I could bring to this role?

- Can you describe a general "day in the life" of this role? How would a successful person divide his time or organize his responsibilities to do it well?

- How will my performance be measured? How will I know if I'm doing a good job, as well as how I can improve?

- If I wanted to work on additional areas of responsibility outside the official role, perhaps for 15 percent of the time, how would you feel about that?

These types of questions accomplish a few different things. First, the answers should be helpful to you, the candidate, in determining if the job is the right fit for you. Second, the questions demonstrate interest—a desire to contribute as well as a wish to assert your independence and autonomy.

For best results, combine a couple of these questions with a couple of your own that are more specific to the company or organization as well as to the skills, interests, and passions that matter most to you.

WORKING SMARTER DOESN'T MEAN NOT WORKING HARD

When 20-year-old Shelli Rae Varela decided to become a firefighter, she counted the cost and figured out exactly what was required. It took several years to get the gig, but she's now done it for more than two decades. There's no doubt about it: this job is what she was born to do.

During one of our interviews, Shelli had to stop abruptly to respond to an emergency call. A patient had been reported as "NVS," having no vital signs. Her crew raced to the scene to help, and by the time they left, the patient had regained a pulse. Catching up later, Shelli told me with obvious joy in her voice how much she loves that this is what she gets to do every day. It isn't an easy job, but that's exactly the point. The work matters, and she feels good about doing it.

For Shelli, the 1,162 days of studying, training, and test taking were worth the effort. How much effort are you willing to put into landing *your* dream job?

"I didn't wait until I knew how to get started, I just got started. I was really scared most of the time, but I've found nothing can replace taking action on a dream. Nobody wants to be known as an idea guy, they want to be known as someone who made things happen."

—HEATH, AGE 24, WRITER AND FILMMAKER

10

The Self-Employed Employee

OBJECTIVE:

Become Indispensable

There's nothing wrong with working for a boss or company, especially if you can make the job work for you. Hack your job by becoming invaluable to the organization—while also crafting the job of your dreams.

When Leon Adato describes his job as a technology evangelist at a software company, he proudly refers to his role and job title as "head geek." "Who wouldn't want a job like mine?" he asked enthusiastically in a response to one of my surveys. When I caught up with him by Skype from his home office in Cleveland, Ohio, to learn more, he explained how he'd come to land the ideal role.

The job of head geek requires him to attend and speak at conferences he would want to attend on his own dime, and to write about topics he was writing about before for free. As you'd probably expect, this dream job didn't come out of nowhere, and the full story began with an early career change.

Leon grew up in Cleveland as the son of a percussionist in the local symphony orchestra. The performing arts were encouraged in his family, and from an early age Leon wanted to be in theater. After graduating from New York University's drama program, he hustled for a while, taking a job at a theater for the deaf that required 70-hour workweeks and paid only $10,000 a year. True, it was theater—and thespians often make sacrifices for the stage—but the lifestyle wasn't compatible with Leon's goals. He wanted a family, and he recognized that his chances of success as an actor were slim.

Unfortunately, a degree in theater didn't qualify Leon for much more than a series of jobs in food service and pest control, which clearly weren't the end goal. But then, while working a temporary gig as an administrative assistant way back in 1988, Leon discovered that he was really good at using computers. He started volunteering to show everyone else in the office how to transition from old-school word processors to the latest PCs, and was soon offered a "real job" teaching software to secretaries full-time.

He felt useful doing this work, even as he prepared for class sessions by reading one page ahead in the manuals he taught from. "Back then," he told me, "there were two requirements for getting a job in computers. One was 'Are you breathing?' and the other was 'Do you own a suit?' One of those was optional."

The software training job lasted five years and was a tremendous learning experience, one in which Leon got paid to master more than a hundred different software programs. Not only was he becoming more and more invaluable to the company, he was also amassing a resumé with a list of skills that was pages long. He also adapted his theater skills to the classroom and said that his daily teaching routine was essentially eight hours of stand-up comedy.

A much more qualified Leon Adato moved up in the world of computers to desktop support, then to server support, and then to the newer world of systems monitoring. He was the guy responsible for ensuring that networks keep running and blocks of computers remain online—a critically important role. He worked another series of jobs, changing companies every two or three years. In many professions it doesn't always look good to job-hop, but in the world of IT, if you *don't* change jobs frequently, employers wonder about your abilities.

Each of these jobs was usually a step forward in terms of income and responsibilities. Among other positions, he worked for Nestlé for a while, setting up a major system for the company in North America and then in Switzerland, where he was relocated with his family for a year.

For many of these years he'd also been working on the side, designing websites for clients and friends, and writing about the evolving world of tech. He joked it was the "midnight to 5:00 a.m. shift," but he preferred doing it as a side gig rather than full-time. Leon was an advocate for telecommuting, and he had enough self-discipline to work on his own, but he also enjoyed being part of a larger organization with other employees.

Leon's dream job appeared on the horizon when he began contributing to a community forum run by Solar-Winds, a software company. After proving himself as a helpful and knowledgeable resource, he took on the paid position of head geek, a unique role he was able to tailor to fit his skills and interests as well as the needs of the company.

Back in his NYU days, Leon had wanted to perform. Now he gets to speak at conferences, a practice he describes as "getting up in front of groups of people and showing off." When he was learning about computers, he wrote and distributed essays just for fun. Now something he used to do for free is part of his job.

Whether everyone wants a job like Leon's may be up for debate, but there's no doubt that he's found the work he was born to do. He avoided having to deal with the risk and uncertainty of quitting his job without a safety net, or trying to turn a side hustle into a full-time business, or starting a business of his own. Instead, he did it by hacking his job to support his ideal lifestyle—while making himself indispensable to his employers at the same time. After having changed jobs every two years for so long, Leon now hopes to stay put awhile.

YOU ARE SELF-EMPLOYED, ONE WAY OR ANOTHER

Stories abound of good people losing good jobs. In today's "gig economy," qualified, hardworking employees are no longer guaranteed lifetime work and pay by any employer. Even government, academic, or other traditionally "safe" jobs aren't so secure these days. I knew a guy who'd been in the military for nearly 20 years and was then laid off with no explanation—right before the government pension would have kicked in.

This means that even if you're earning a steady paycheck, you are essentially self-employed in terms of being responsible for your own career. Therefore, you should continually build your skills and look out for yourself. This is important for two big reasons: first, to safeguard your current position, and second, as a means of advancement.

In Leon's career, he was able to advance through several different roles at several different companies by upgrading his skills and seeking to contribute more than what was expected. These efforts paid off, ultimately making him so indispensable to his new employers that they let him custom-design the position he wanted.

Most people tend to think that to be an entrepreneur, you have to start a social network in your basement or build a computer company in your garage. But that couldn't be further from the truth. These days you don't even need to start a company to call yourself an entrepreneur; you can be just as entrepreneurial within a traditional company or organization. The trick is to do as Leon did and design a position that allows you to embrace your interests and be as innovative as you could be if you were *actually* self-employed.

But how? It all comes down to becoming indispensable to your current employer. When your team, company, or business simply can't function without you, you'll have the best bargaining chip in the world when you come to your boss asking him to let you design your lottery-winning role. Indispensability isn't available merely for the asking, but you can build it over time by adapting the four strategies listed below.

BE THE INDISPENSABLE EMPLOYEE: FOUR STRATEGIES

Strategy #1: Keep the Trains Running on Time

Everyone knows someone who goes above and beyond in the workplace. This person gets the job done, sure—but beyond just completing the basics, this person seeks to help out wherever needed.

For example, from time to time you'll arrive at a meeting where it's not clear who's in charge. When this hap-

GATE	TIME	DESTINATION	STATUS
B13	11:00	**KEEP**	ON TIME
A26	12:45	**THE**	ON TIME
A40	2:00	**TRAINS**	ON TIME
A28	4:15	**RUNNING**	ON TIME

pens, assess the situation to determine the leadership skills of the other attendees. Remember that your goal is to get things done and make other people look good. Then, take the initiative without taking control. Be helpful, ask questions, and offer to accept tasks on behalf of the group.

At the end of the meeting, provide a quick wrap-up based on the actions the group agreed to: "Okay, so John will call the supplier to check on delivery, I'll do the other research and report back," and so on. Finally, if no one else is openly taking notes, do it yourself. Type them up and send them out to the participants within 24 hours of the meeting.

You may have heard the saying "If you want to get something done, ask a busy person to do it." To be indispensable, be the busy person who gets things done—and keeps other things on track for the rest of the group.

Strategy #2: Prevent Rent-Seeking and Other Bad Behavior in the Workplace

If you've ever held any sort of job, or even if you're self-employed, you're probably aware that not every moment of "working hours" is highly productive. In fact, much of it is unproductive. It's hard to remove unproductive work *completely*, as there will always be a certain amount of unavoidable slippage in our daily tasks and meetings. Most unproductive work, however, is simply the result of a common bad habit of people taking on work to make themselves look good or enhance their stature without adding any real value.

Economists refer to activities that seek to transfer wealth without increasing value as "rent-seeking." It's what lobbyists do in trying to convince government leaders to throw contracts their way. It's also what dispensable employees do when they occupy themselves with pointless tasks on company time. No matter what kind of jobs you've had, you can probably think of your own examples of this practice.

I experienced an extreme case of rent-seeking when I traveled across the border between Benin and Nigeria in West Africa. Nigeria is a beautiful country with many friendly people, but most of them would be the first to tell you that the government there is incredibly corrupt. Bribes are essentially a means of doing business and a normal part of daily life. At that point I'd been living in West Africa, where corruption is endemic, for a couple of years. Even so, I was shocked at the scope and brazenness of the requests I received on this border crossing. To make it through, I had to present my passport to no fewer than eight different guys, who were all lined up in an open-air office. Presumably they were all there to fulfill an important function, but I couldn't tell what it was. Some of them waved me by without a word, others asked a question or two, and some

PREVENT
RENT-SEEKING
BEHAVIOR

TASKS
☑ ZERO-VALUE
☑ TIME-WASTER
☑ CIRCULAR

simply held on to my passport and waited for me. As far as I could tell, none was accomplishing anything other than intimidating travelers and attempting to extract extra payments.

Hopefully you don't encounter this level of rent-seeking in your office. There may be times, however, when you notice an activity taking place that is inherently circular or doesn't advance the goals of the organization. Wherever possible, work against this behavior—and take care to ensure you don't give in to the temptation to indulge in it yourself.

Strategy #3: Help Your Organization Achieve Its Key Goals, Even If They Don't Directly Relate to Your Actual Job

There are many different roles in a large enterprise, and not all of them are directly responsible for bringing in income or achieving other tangible goals. You may be a critical part of behind-the-scenes work, but find a way to go even further. Don't just be a hard worker; find a way to boost profits or otherwise draw a direct connection between your efforts and the greater success of the organization.

I once knew an aid worker who was responsible for raising his own financial support for the charity organization he volunteered with full-time. Every quarter he'd write letters to his supporters, thanking them for their help while gently reminding them of ongoing needs. The challenge was that this person was an accountant for the organization—one of those critical roles that doesn't necessarily sound exciting to outsiders. In an attempt to inspire more contributions, he figured out a creative way to describe his work. Instead of writing about his day-to-day responsibilities, which involved balancing figures and spending a lot of time staring at spreadsheets, he told the greater story of what the organization itself was doing. He then talked about how the support roles that he and his co-workers fulfilled contributed to those larger goals. "This is what you're making happen!" was the implied statement, and it was highly effective.

HELP YOUR ORGANIZATION
ACHIEVE ITS GOALS

Strategy #4: If Your Work Is in Danger of Becoming Obsolete, Don't Hang On for Dear Life—Change It Up!

Every year I look on in disbelief as stacks of printed telephone directories are delivered outside my office. And every year I watch as tenant after tenant immediately throws the directory into the recycle bin (I do the same). The rest of the 500-page paperweights are left sitting in the lobby until someone finally shows up to remove them, presumably to a landfill or at least a recycling center.

Not only is this practice incredibly wasteful, it's also an obvious sign of a business on the verge of extinction. Cell phones are the new landlines, yet hundreds of thousands of these useless telephone directories continue to be printed. Presumably the phone book business continues because advertisers are still willing to pay to support it, but once the advertisers stop paying, the business will end.

Imagine that you're in charge of operations for one of the companies that makes printed telephone directories. What would you do? First of all, you may want to immediately start looking for another job. But assuming you're relatively happy, you'd do well to think about how you could help bring this increasingly irrelevant product back to life, or at least support the industry's transition to something that makes more sense in modern times.

No matter your industry or employer, ask these questions about the business and consider what you can do to support positive change:

- Will people still want our products and services in five years?

- How can our business continue to be relevant in changing times?

- What can we do to build for the future?

FROM CONSULTANT TO STARTUP TO EMPLOYEE, ON HER OWN TERMS

Even if you don't value the traditional benefits of a traditional job (steady paycheck, benefits, some degree of security), there are plenty of careers that you can't pursue as a solo artist. Shelli Rae Varela, the firefighter you heard about in the previous chapter, is a great example. You simply can't be a solo firefighter, no matter how hard you try. The key is to hack that job to make it work for you—and you'll probably become a better employee in the process.

Chiara Cokieng grew up in the Philippines and always wanted to do something on her own. All around her, she noticed micro-entrepreneurs making money in creative ways—ordinary people who made a living selling goods in the market or driving jeepneys—and the lifestyle appealed to her. She was entrepreneurial by nature, and had discovered her first business opportunity as a young marble distributor way back in elementary school. Chiara realized she could purchase marbles in bulk for only one peso each (2¢) and resell them for five pesos (10¢), pocketing the difference as profit.

After graduating from a prestigious program at the University of the Philippines, she went to work for a global consulting firm, the tried-and-true path of the country's elite graduates. The job was interesting and it allowed her to travel to the United States for several months. Her assignment was in Atlanta, but she used her weekends to visit San Francisco, New York, and other cities. This was fun for a while, but when she'd fly back to the client's office on Sunday night or Monday night, Chiara was often in the company of other consultants en route to their week's assignments. Many of them looked miserable to her, and she decided that the experience wasn't what she wanted to do for the long term.

Chiara had been reading up and plotting out a plan for a new copywriting business she planned to launch, and once she was back in the Philippines, she took the leap. In an act of faith, she prematurely wrote a rather optimistic blog post entitled "How I Quit My Job and Doubled My Income." The only problem was, the second part didn't actually happen. Her copywriting business wasn't a flop—she gained several clients right away and began building an online following— but it also wasn't the overnight success she'd dreamed of.

She found something better after she reached out to a mentor for advice. The mentor had founded an interesting company that wasn't like the big consulting agency she'd worked for before, but it was definitely much larger than a tiny one-woman shop. All of a sudden, she knew that she wanted to help grow his business, both to make it successful on its own and also to prepare herself for another attempt at entrepreneurship.

"I'd like to help you with something," she said to her mentor. "If it works out, maybe you'll hire me."

"Okay," he said. "But what's the 'something'?"

On a whim, Chiara said that she had some ideas to improve the company's website analytics. As to how she'd do it, that was a learn-on-the-job process: she took her initial objectives from the online listing for a book about analytics. She learned quickly, and then *just did it* without waiting for official permission or even a verbal guarantee that the work would lead to a job. Her bet paid off. Before much longer, the company's founder created a full-time job for her, with completely flexible hours.

Two years later, she continues to support the startup. But she's also got her eye on the next iteration of the business. In the long run, she wants to accomplish both goals: to help the startup achieve scale, and to return to her own business ideas.

SHOW PROOF OF CONCEPT

Once you've made yourself invaluable to your boss or employer, how do you convince the higher-ups to let you hack your existing job into the work you were born to do?

Chiara's strategy was to present "proof of concept"—she showed a potential employer exactly what she was capable of doing, simply by doing it. She also related that proof directly to the value that she could bring.

She didn't ask for permission, or even wait until she'd been formally hired. Instead, she took the initiative to jump right in and demonstrate the value that she could bring to the company, and it worked. This is a strategy that can be effective for you whether you're trying to get hired by your dream employer or to shift responsibilities in your current job. Put simply, if you can prove that you're indispensable at something, why *wouldn't* your boss or employer want you to take it on?

BE THE RIGHT KIND OF HERO

Once upon a time I lived in the small country of Togo in West Africa. I was based on a hospital ship docked in Lomé, the capital city, and was part of a team that had an educational project three hours north in a village.

Lori, one of our team members, needed to be at the village during the week, but not over the weekend. Because we had a lot of projects competing for transportation, we couldn't allocate a vehicle specifically to her. She could have stayed in the village over the weekend, but life in the village gets old after a few days. What to do?

I solved the problem by offering to drive her both ways for as long as she needed. This way the vehicle would be available for others during the week, but she wouldn't have to stay in the village for all those extra days.

"That's crazy!" another colleague said when he heard about my idea. "You can't drive six hours round-trip twice a week for three months."

But that's what I did, and it wasn't that hard. All I had to do was . . . drive.

Week in and week out, I drove a Land Rover three hours north, dropped Lori off, then drove back on my own. On Thursdays I'd make the return trip, picking her up and delivering both of us back to the ship.

To me it seemed simple enough: something needed doing, I didn't see another way to do it, so I just did it myself.

Was I a hero? In some ways I was *helpful*, and my intentions were good, but in retrospect this may not have been the smartest decision. By being "so helpful" to her, I was unavailable for other people during those hours. Some of my regular tasks were left undone, and because I was always tired when I returned from the six-hour round trip, it interfered with my ability to be productive.

Sure, making the drive a couple of times was great—it's always good to support your team and be the first one to volunteer. But maybe instead of driving her myself every time, I could have figured something else out. I could have recruited a couple of other volunteers, so we could share the load. I could have done some fund-raising to hire a car and driver for some of the trips, so that one of us wouldn't have to take six hours away from the other crucial work.

> You want to be reliable and indispensable. The real
> heroes, though, are able to see the bigger picture and
> come up with solutions that are truly good for every-
> one involved.

"HEY, BOSS, LET'S TALK ABOUT PRIORITIES: YOURS AND MINE"

Becoming indispensable is great, but it comes with one big challenge. Once you're a trusted and valued employee, your bosses may begin to want you to take on more and more tasks. When the time comes to consider yet another project or responsibility, it may be better to ask the people you work with (and work for) to consider the request in light of the other responsibilities you're already carrying.

Framing the conversation in a "Let me help you" manner is best. Your boss or colleagues may not be aware of everything you're already doing, so be sure you come prepared with a list. Here's a good opening sentence: "I'm currently working on a couple of other high-priority projects. Which of these priorities is most important to you?"

You can also ask for additional resources to do the job well. Try this approach: "Okay, I understand this is important, but I have a bunch of other things happening as well. For me to do this new thing, here's what I'll need."

Lastly, point out the positive potential of taking on the task in a way that allows others to be involved as well. This might help: "Do you want me to handle this whole task on my own, or should I find a way to do it that allows for someone else to do it in the future?"

In the end, your goal of becoming an indispensable employee will work only if you don't get overwhelmed to the point of not being helpful at all. Be sure you can do everything in your current portfolio with excellence before raising your hand to volunteer for a ton of other stuff.

TAKE A SABBATICAL, EVEN IF YOU STAY ON THE JOB

Sometimes you know exactly what your dream role at your current job or company is. Other times you might not be so sure. What then?

You may be familiar with the concept of a sabbatical, where you take an extended break from your job, either to rest completely or to pursue something very different before returning. A sabbatical can be a great way to reboot and recharge, so you come back to work energized and raring to go. It can also be a great opportunity to reflect on what's not working for you in your current role, gain some perspective, and maybe do some experimentation to figure out what changes you can make to turn your current job into the work you were born to do. Professors, for example, often take sabbaticals so they can focus on conducting research or publishing in their field. Traditional sabbaticals are usually anywhere from one month to three months or longer, and they can be hard to come by these days. Even so, some people are finding ways to incorporate longer breaks into their job commitments.

Rachael O'Meara, a longtime Google employee, was struggling in her work performance. She still believed in the company's mission, and the working conditions were great, but she needed a break. She approached her manager with a request: "Can I take three months of unpaid leave?" It wasn't an easy sell, but Rachael explained that she was committed to Google and planned to return, she just needed some time away first. After some discussion with HR, the request was approved on the condition that she train a replacement before taking off.

During her sabbatical, she deliberately didn't plan any big activities. She took a couple of small trips with friends and family, then settled into a friend's rental home in Tahoe. She spent the time decompressing and completing a series of online courses with the goal of finding something she loved that she was also good at. In the last week of her sabbatical, she went to Burning Man, the annual gathering of arts and culture in the Nevada desert. Upon returning to Google, she took on an entirely new role as an account executive in the sales department, feeling refreshed and recharged.

In Alexandria, Virginia, a personal finance advisory company has an unconventional sabbatical practice of its own. The Motley Fool, which has around 300 employees, sends one of them on a "mandatory vacation" every month. In keeping with the company's culture, it's called a "Fool's Errand," and each month the lucky employee is chosen by lottery (with long-term workers receiving multiple entries based on their number of years of service). The winner gets two weeks off and $1,000 to spend however they like, but there's one strict rule: the employee must leave immediately and have no contact with the office while gone. Winners are also encouraged to do something that contributes to the Motley Fool's overall mission ("to help the world invest better"), but aside from not checking work email or phoning in to conference calls, there's no restriction on what people can do.

You may not have such a generous and flexible award available to you, but maybe this story can inspire you to propose a similar program at your company. Is there a Fool's Errand of your own you'd like to undertake? If it's not possible to do it for two weeks, could you take off work to do something different for just a single day?

Lastly, if an out-of-office sabbatical isn't in the cards for you right now, consider an *in-house sabbatical*, where you try out another role or set of responsibilities. You could ask to shadow people working in other roles, or even try to get permission to join another department or division for a week. During this time, you'll gain an understanding of how things work in other departments or positions, possibly sparking ideas you can tailor to your own.

As always, the more value you contribute to the organization, the easier it will be for you to negotiate a favorable arrangement. It may be hard for your boss to survive without you for a while, but if you remind her you'll come back rested and more indispensable than ever, a smart boss will realize that your proposal is a win-win for everyone.

Leon, Rachael, and others became invaluable employees and were able to hack their jobs into positions that met their ideal intersection of passion, skill, and flow. They also created much more job security for themselves, whether in their current roles or in the form of additional opportunities.

There's nothing wrong with being an employee, especially when you make the job work for you.

"Some people would look at my resumé and see chaos. My dad's best friend said early that he'd never hire me because I've jumped around so much. But to me it makes perfect sense. I never fit the corporate mold or the 9-to-5 office way. By creating my own career, I can grow and expand, which I believe allows me to serve others and myself more fully."

—LIA, AGE 44, INDEPENDENT BRAND CONSULTANT

11

DIY Rock Star

OBJECTIVE:

Recruit a Small Army of Fans and Supporters

There used to be a saying among artists that their success was due "to the fans." Yet the musicians, artists, and writers who thrive today understand that their success is due not only "to the fans" but also to the relationship the artist maintains with the fans. Here's how to become an independent rock star at any creative endeavor by creating a loyal fan base in the new world order (leather pants not included).

244 BORN FOR THIS

When I was younger, I used to play music. I played a lot of instruments, always trying to pick up a new skill, but bass and piano were my favorites. I played reasonably well, and I tried to be a good listener when playing with a group. I learned to read music and improvise, two skills that don't always go together in the music world, and I was somewhat reliable when a bandleader called me for a gig.

Nevertheless, I wasn't great. Just as I had to accept that I'd never become a pro basketball player, I also came to terms with the fact that Katy Perry wouldn't be calling me to join her in the studio anytime soon.

But eventually I realized that my dreams of becoming a rock star weren't really about wanting to spend my days recording music in a windowless studio. What I really wanted was to *tour*. I wanted to go on the road. I'd always loved travel, even before I set out to properly see the world, and I loved the idea of going city to city, one stop after another, soaking up the different sights during the day and performing to crowds in the evenings.

I didn't need groupies or bowls of M&Ms, and I didn't need it to be glamorous. I just wanted to connect with people in different places, and I was drawn to a lifestyle of changing scenery.

I gave up playing music when I started writing, but a funny thing happened: I actually ended up getting everything that I originally wanted. True, Katy Perry never called, but I found my way to the work I was meant to do.

It just developed in a very different way than I first expected.

279 DAYS TO OVERNIGHT SUCCESS

For the past seven years I've made a good living as an independent writer. I chronicled the first year of this journey in an online manifesto, "279 Days to Overnight Success." As I said at the time, this was the story of creating a new, full-time income as a writer, without any ads or sponsors on my site. Much of that earlier story is still relevant, and after more than two million downloads it continues to be freely available on my website.

The "279 Days" manifesto wasn't really a culmination of anything; it was simply a chronology of what had happened on my journey thus far. This journey continued long after I wrote the initial story, as I visited at least 20 countries a year, writing about my adventures and connecting with more readers and interesting people wherever I went. When I wrote at the time that I was thrilled about making a decent living through independent writing, it was true—but I was even more excited about the "next chapter" of writing books and going on the road.

Fast-forward to 2010, where I was getting ready for my first book to come out. I'd been traveling actively for several years at that point, and the blog was growing in readership every week.

I knew that this developing community was only as strong as my connection with the people who read and participated, so I decided to meet as many of them as I could on an independent tour of all 50 U.S. states and all 10 Canadian provinces. I added in a couple of other stops for a grand total of 63, and sent out a call for readers to help organize an "unconventional book tour."

The tour was a great success. All along the way, I met people who showed up with interesting stories, sometimes having driven several hours to attend. I gave a brief talk and then did Q&A at every stop, but I tried to make most events less focused on the book and more on the *people*.

Among other places, I gathered with groups of readers in a Pilates studio (New Haven), coffee shops (Wilmington, Lexington, and Louisville), a pizza parlor (Anchorage), a bed-and-breakfast (Atlanta), an art gallery (Lawrence), a farm (Nashville), a heavy metal concert hall (San Francisco), a corporate office building (Philadelphia), and numerous co-working spaces.

The weirdest gig of all was in a grocery store in downtown Minneapolis. The venue wasn't as off-the-wall as it initially sounds: the store was part of a neighborhood revitalization effort, and it was surrounded by lots of interesting ethnic food shops. However, it was still a *grocery store*, with terrible acoustics and a stage set up right across from the frozen foods section. Nearby shoppers who had come in for a gallon of milk and had no idea what was going on mingled with my readers who'd come out for the event. Once in a while, an announcement would come over the PA, interrupting my talk: "Ladies and gentlemen, we have two-for-one pound cake back in the bakery. There's also a special on cauliflower!"

After that experience, I made a resolution: no more grocery stores.

But I kept trucking along, doing whatever I could to build traction for my books and support the growing community. I knew that as long as I continued to write and produce work that people valued enough to pay for, I could never be fired—and I could go on tour whenever I wanted. Even without the bowls of M&Ms, I felt like I had found my inner rock star.

SKIP REALITY TV TRYOUTS, BUILD YOUR OWN FAN BASE

To become a successful musician in the "old days," you had to be anointed or recognized by a gatekeeper, usually a record label. The same was true for authors: to be successful, your main goal was to convince a publisher to take a risk on you. Similarly, visual artists needed galleries, and radio hosts needed stations.

Talent wasn't enough, in other words. Even if you had a proven means of providing something valuable to an audience, you still had to rely on the powers that be to help you reach that audience.

Fortunately, times have changed in the world of stardom. Today, thanks to mediums like Instagram and Twitter that make engaging and communicating with fans easier than ever, more and more people are carving out a space for their independent, fan-supported work. Indie musicians often choose to go it alone, even after they have the opportunity to sign with labels. Traditional publishers are now scrambling to sign authors who have sold hundreds of thousands of books direct to readers through Amazon's Kindle platform, or sometimes even directly through their own websites.

The musicians, artists, and writers who thrive today understand that their success is due not only "to the fans," which is something that artists have always said. The difference is that now success is due to *the relationship the artist maintains with the fans.*

I could tell you success stories for days. A few of my favorites:

- The novelist Robin Sloan self-published a story that became a bestselling book when it was adopted by thousands of eager readers

- The indie band Pomplamoose racked up hundreds of millions of views on YouTube and then self-produced a 28-city tour (more on them in a moment)

- The French-American painter Gwenn Seemel releases all of her work under a free license, yet still earns a good living from the portraits she specializes in

There's a lot to learn from these examples, but let's get an important disclaimer out of the way: with creative and artistic pursuits in particular, success is never directly replicable in the sense that you can do exactly what these people did and see exactly the same results.

However, if you're seeking a similar kind of success, it's also important to understand what the success stories have in common. Fortunately, the answer is very clear. Almost without exception, those who succeed in the new economy share four specific characteristics: a body of work (product), a group of fans (audience), a means of sharing the body of work (platform), and a way of getting paid for their work (money).

The Product

Every artist has a portfolio, a body of work that she makes for others to consume. This doesn't have to be "art" in the traditional sense; it can include any number of things such as paintings, podcasts, essays, educational resources, downloadable singles, albums, handmade jewelry, branded merchandise, funny cat photos (there's a market for everything . . .), and many other options. Any successful artist knows to be focused most of all on expanding and developing her body of work.

The Audience

A brilliant portfolio is worth nothing without fans, the people who appreciate—and, crucially, support—the artist's work. Aspiring artists often struggle with gaining fans, and it's easy to become frustrated. Gaining fans is not a simple process; you can't just run out to the fan store and pick up a 12-pack. It requires patience, persistence, and authentic, two-way engagement. The most popular artists are the ones who communicate *with* their fans, not *at* them.

Over time, however, if you can consistently and authentically connect and engage with people who appreciate what you create and want to be part of it in some way, you'll gain and maintain a loyal following of fans, evangelists, and ambassadors who will not only devour your work but eagerly spread the word to others.

The Platform

To build this following, you'll need a platform, a means of connecting with fans on a regular or at least semi-regular basis. These days, "platform" tends to refer to an active following on social media, or perhaps to an email or other newsletter list. But this focus on relatively new technology should not be thought of as exclusive or complete. Long ago, decades before social media, many smart artists, writers, and musicians still had a platform. Another way to think of a platform is as a way to reach people who care about your work. There's more than one possible way, but you can't skip this requirement entirely.

The Marketplace

Finally—and this is key—successful DIY rock stars have a way for fans to pay to support their work. Again, there are many different ways of getting paid, but if your endeavor is a career plan instead of a hobby, somehow you need to create at least one recurring method of getting money into your bank account.

The easiest and most common way to get paid is simply

to sell the body of work directly to fans and other interested people. Other people find more creative solutions, however. The musician and performance artist Amanda Palmer, for example, is famous for (among other things) having raised more than $1 million in a crowdfunding campaign for a new album. She credits the relationships she's diligently built with fans over the years as the most important factor in the success of the campaign, which never would have caught on if it weren't for the buzz that originated from that base.

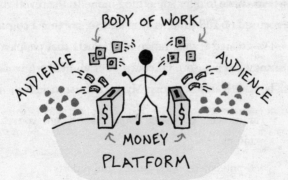

None of these four requirements is optional; you need all of them to succeed in the new economy. It can be tempting to cherry-pick an example of someone famous who's made it big by omitting something listed above, but those are the very rare exceptions. If you're hoping to follow the proven model, you need all four requirements.

DON'T JUST BE INSPIRING; CREATE THINGS THAT PEOPLE CAN BUY

Remember, fans will connect with you in different ways, and they want to support people they care about. If your goal is to make a living, though, you obviously need to create something they can buy. Figuring out what that is will be obvious for some people. If you're a musician, you make music; if you're a painter, you make paintings.

Sometimes, however, to make a real livable income as an artist, you have to offer something more. In the seven years I've focused on full-time writing and supporting a community, I've created a wide range of products that people can consume (and pay for). Of course, not all of them worked well, but that's another story. My partial list includes:

- Traditionally published books (like the one you're reading)
- Self-published books, guides, and reports
- A "travel hacking" membership site, where I help readers earn frequent flyer miles and travel the world
- A year-long marketing course
- Various other online courses
- Affiliate relationships with travel providers and entrepreneurial resources
- In-person events (although in my case, most of those tend to operate on a not-for-profit model)

- Some things I've forgotten or better left unsaid (again, not everything works!)

One more disclaimer: this list may feel like some sort of diabolical plan to get rich, but it's really not. Each of these offerings has emerged naturally and evolved over time as I've tried to pay attention to a) the needs of the community, and b) how those needs overlap with what I can provide. I know several other writers who are much more active than me in building out a complete "funnel" of products and services. I have only one assistant and prefer to spend more time writing and traveling. As a result, there are many opportunities I don't pursue that may be ideal for other people. I don't sell coaching or consulting services, for example, and I have no sponsors or advertisers.

That's just one of the benefits of being a DIY rock star— *you* get to choose your own business model. As for those offerings that totally bombed, well, there's a time and place for those, too. Sometimes it's worth it to lose money in the short term in support of a greater long-term goal.

COME OUT AHEAD BY LOSING MONEY

On that first book tour of mine, where I went to every U.S. state and Canadian province, I lost money. So too did Pomplamoose in the indie tour mentioned above (the band spent $147,802 and had income of $135,983, for a net loss of $11,819). You'd be right to think that losing money is not an

254 BORN FOR THIS

optimal goal, even for artists. But the whole story for both of these experiences is that success is found in the long-term value, not just the short-term profit or loss.

Here's what Jack Conte, the co–front man of Pomplamoose, had to say about it: "We knew it would be an expensive endeavor, and we still chose to make the investment. We could have played a duo show instead of hiring six people to tour with us. That would have saved us over $50,000, but it was important at this stage in Pomplamoose's career to put on a wild and crazy rock show. We wanted to be invited back to every venue, and we wanted our fans to bring their friends next time. The loss was an investment in future tours."

How's that for a long-term perspective? I felt much the same way on that first big tour of my own. In that experience, my accounting wasn't nearly as detailed as Jack's (remember, there's a reason I changed majors); but as best as I could tell, the expenses were about $30,000, and since admission to all events was free, there was no direct income.

Yet it wasn't a true loss, either in the crucial long-term building of an audience or in the short-term growth of my business. Like Pomplamoose, I believed it was an investment in building a community, not just a one-off expense.[*]

---

[*] To be clear, I don't think you should make these kinds of investments in a side hustle or an experiment. If you aren't fully committed to the idea or project, save your money. When you believe in something so much that you're willing to sacrifice for it, that's when you decide to invest.

ALWAYS FOCUS ON MAKING SOMETHING THAT MATTERS

At least once a year I travel to Dubai, a place I always enjoy visiting. But one thing about the place always perplexes me. Time after time, I've been to beautiful restaurants filled with opulent place settings and an eager staff of servers— yet very few customers to fill the tables, and sometimes none at all. Those restaurants put so much time and effort into providing a special experience for diners, and yet the diners don't come. So why do these restaurant owners continue to do it? That's a subject for another book, but the point is that it's much better to be in the opposite position, where not everything is shiny and perfect and you don't have all the details figured out—but you're making something you believe in for a growing community of people who care enough to show up.

When diners love a new restaurant, it doesn't matter if the place settings are chipped or if the line is an hour long. You can always polish up or improve things as you go along. What matters is that the people—the fans— come out.

If you get a few big things right, in other words, you can get a lot of small things wrong. Don't put all your attention on the trappings of being the rock star. Focus instead on making something that matters and connecting with people who get what it's all about.

THE PROFESSIONAL REINVENTIONIST

Whenever he went through security at an airport, Jason had a problem: which ID should he use? He had to remember when he bought the ticket, since that would likely indicate which last name he had provided at the time.

It sounds shady, but Jason wasn't a criminal; he had simply auctioned off the rights to his last name. For an entire year, he was Jason HeadsetsDotCom—an actual, legal name, but obviously not the one he had been given by his parents. Then, for another year after that, he was Jason SurfrApp, another name that doesn't show up on most birth certificates. How did this come about? As you might expect, there's a story.

Unless they're taking on the name of a spouse, most adults stick with the name they've had since day one. Jason, though, legally changed his name three times in a few short years.

He had always been up for crazy experiments. After finishing college in Florida, Jason worked for several years as a graphic designer in a ho-hum job. As he saw countless companies struggling to get their message out, he had an idea: what if he offered his services as a free-range advertiser for any company willing to pay? He called the concept "I Wear Your Shirt," which did exactly what it promised. Every day for an entire year, Jason would wear a different company's T-shirt and actively promote them on social media.

On January 1, 2009, the project began. The first day's shirt cost $1, the second day's $2, and so on—all the way up to the $365 price on the last day of the year. As word got out, companies booked slots months in advance, and then for the following year at a higher price. For nearly five years, Jason continued the project, wearing *thousands* of T-shirts and extolling brands ranging from tiny businesses no one had heard of to big companies like Nike and Nissan. The project went well, bringing in $80,000 the first year, and then much more for the next four years—but what would he do next? Jason didn't want to wear sponsored T-shirts every day for the rest of his life. That's when he hit on the next big idea: to auction off the rights to his last name.

First, some background. Jason had grown up without a stable father figure. A series of stepfathers had left Jason with different last names, none of which he felt particularly attached to. If you don't love your name, he thought, why not get a new one?

Crazy marketer that he was, Jason decided to change his name to whatever the highest bidder wanted to pay. He launched a new site, BuyMyLastName.com, and held an online auction. The winner was Headsets.com, a startup that had a history of producing zany stunts of its own. "We once offered free headsets for life to anyone who tattooed our name on their bodies," the CEO said, "so this seemed like a natural extension."

Headsets.com paid $45,500 for Jason to become Jason HeadsetsDotCom. As funny as it sounds, the change was real—Jason *legally* changed his name, updating his photo ID and as many official documents as he could. In this day and age, those updates included social media accounts, where thousands of people interacted with him every day.

He repeated the experiment one year later, changing his last name to SurfrApp, sold for $50,000 to another startup where people document and share their surfing adventures.

I'd heard of Jason's antics, but I started paying more attention when a book he'd written, *Creativity for Sale*, landed on my desk. The plan for the book project borrowed from his other campaigns: when he wanted to write a book, he sold $75,000 worth of sponsorships, including a different package *for every page*. The memoir and field manual is surprisingly interesting for a book that includes a footnoted advertisement on all 224 of its pages.

Whether his last name was Sadler, HeadsetsDotCom, SurfrApp, or Zook (a great-grandfather's name he eventually settled on as a final choice for the rest of his life), I was fascinated by the stream of ideas and projects that I saw from Jason. These days, you might hear of a project like Jason's every week . . . but you don't usually hear of project after project from the same person.

The theme that ran through Jason's work was "where opportunity meets action"—something I thought a lot about in the writing of this book. All of Jason's zany ideas were opportunities that other people had passed by but which Jason decided to actually pursue. Any one idea was interesting and fun, but it was the *culmination* of ideas and the ability to evolve that made Jason successful in the long term. And the ideas weren't only creative; they also provided a service that someone wanted.

LOCAL VS. GLOBAL: CHOOSE ONE

Derek Sivers is another DIY rock star who built a multimillion-dollar retail business on a highly unusual strategy: answer the phone when customers call. He later went on to sell the business, giving most of the profits to a foundation before pursuing a number of other endeavors.

At one point in his peripatetic life, he was living in Singapore while building a new website. Derek had given a number of popular TED talks and was a minor celebrity among aspiring entrepreneurs, and almost every day he received requests to have coffee, lunch, or drinks. He said yes to as many of these requests as possible, and he usually enjoyed the meetings—but pretty soon he realized they were causing a problem. He was spending so much time drinking and dining that he had no time left to build the new business, one that would serve a global audience of thousands. He realized that he faced a choice, and it wasn't unique to him.

Here's how he put it:

> You can focus your time locally *or* globally. But if you over-commit yourself locally, you under-commit yourself globally, and vice versa.
>
> If you're local, then you're probably social, doing a lot of things in person, and being a part of your community. But this means you'll have less time to focus on creating things for the world.
>
> If you're global, then you want to focus on

creating things that can reach out through distribution to the whole world. But this means
you'll have less time to be part of your local
community.

Neither is right or wrong, but you need to be
aware of the choices you're making.

In my work I try to focus on both global and local
impact, with more overall weight toward global, but
I understand exactly what Derek means. None of us
will be able to be fully present in both spheres, so it's
important to decide what matters to you the most.

Jason's story shows that it's possible to go it alone and
find success in a wide range of creative endeavors. As a
modern-day artist—whether that art is music, writing,
food, photography, dance, painting, or something else—
you can build a career based on direct relationships with
fans. Not only that, you can make a good living doing it,
especially if you supplement what you earn from your core
creative work with any number of other income streams.

The best part is that no one can take it away. After all,
if the business is supported entirely by fans and readers,
you can't be fired or laid off. And as Pomplamoose and any
other number of independent artists would tell you, few
things in life are more rewarding than getting paid to create and share something you've made with the world.

Of course, you still have to buy your own leather pants.

"It was the perfect intersection of all the things I enjoy."

—RICHARD, AGE 33, ACUPUNCTURIST

12

How to Do Everything You Want

OBJECTIVE:

Refuse to Choose

Somewhere along the way, you were given some terrible advice: you have to choose a niche. You can safely place this advice in the paper shredder underneath your desk. There may come a time in your career when you need (and want) to focus on one thing, but until it arrives, you can craft the work you were meant to do around all your passions and interests.

When I talked with Devin Gadulet, a 49-year-old editorial director from Los Angeles, he warned me that his career journey would be hard to explain. In the past three decades, he'd owned an antique store, been a professional poker player, worked in the film industry, dabbled in real estate, and started a travel blog at least five years before most people knew what blogs were. He also had a rather unique side project of getting married 100 times—to the same woman, but in as many different locations as possible.

He was right to have warned me. Despite my copious note taking, I had a hard time keeping up with the chronology of all these experiences, so I went with another approach: "When you were eight years old, what did you want to be when you grew up?"

People often have interesting answers to this question. In Devin's case, he responded right away: "I wanted to be the first baseman for the Dodgers," he said. Unfortunately, the baseball dream died in the trauma of turning 12, when he discovered—to much regret—that he wasn't actually cut out for sports.

Throughout middle school, high school, and junior college, he stopped thinking about baseball and started hustling at a variety of projects, jobs, and ventures. He had a lemonade stand, the classic entrepreneurial entry point. He sold comic books and offered tutoring for money.

This energy and ambition stayed with him as he transitioned to adulthood and continued working at a variety of ventures and projects. When his parents divorced, his dad left behind the keys to the family antique store. Devin took over with the classic goal of "buy low, sell high." He learned how to price antiques, and gained an eye for spotting the rare valuable item in a roomful of junk. That was fun for a while, and then he got his first job in the film industry, which led to another, and then another.

Years later, in yet another transition, he established one of the world's first travel blogs and announced a goal to see the world. Few people knew anything about the new world of online media back then, so Devin gave himself the title of editor in chief—as well as senior writer, copyeditor, web designer, tech support, and "guy who does everything else." His success with the blog led to contacts in the travel industry along with invitations for sponsored camera equipment and free trips around the world.

As he recounted all the twists and turns of this unique career journey, Devin described his process of moving from job to job as a spiritual path as much as a career one.

"At the time," he told me, "everything felt like random nonsense. I walked through open doors. I worked in sales for a while and pounded on the phone. . . . I couldn't do that now, but I don't completely regret it. Some of those jobs were things I needed to do to be where I am now.

"I think what I did well," he continued, "was that I had the innocence of youth, and I kept that going for far longer than most people do." He wasn't afraid to try different things—or at least, if he *was* afraid, he didn't let that stop him.

I liked Devin's story, and the more I pressed him for

intel on how he made different choices along the way, the more he went back to the spiritual, philosophical perspective he relied on. "When you're in a vacuum," he said, "you don't always know what you want or what's best. You can make a list of pros and cons, but that doesn't work for everyone or for every situation."

He mentioned a quote he'd heard from a friend: "You have a misguided notion of what you think will make you happy." During this period of his life, Devin had been recovering from what he called a series of "unsuccesses," or ventures that didn't pan out as well as he'd hoped. These dead ends led to a change in perspective. Instead of looking to outside circumstances for happiness, he adopted a view of accepting life in its present state, always seeking to improve but refusing to get hung up on the pursuit of money or status.

These days he continues to work on the travel site, which provides numerous opportunities to travel for free at the behest of tourist boards. He still works in real estate from time to time, and he's also been writing a book. Oh, and he found something else that made him truly happy. Two years ago, Devin married his wife, Morgana Rae, an entrepreneur with a diverse career history of her own. A few months later, they were in Mexico for one of Devin's work assignments. On a whim, he asked her during a walk, "Hey . . . want to get married again?"

She said yes (which was good, since they were already married), and they had their second wedding in Puerto Vallarta. After that, it became a quest: to get married 100 times in worldwide destinations. At the time we spoke, Devin and Morgana had completed 12 weddings in locales including San Marino, Croatia, and Turkey.

Devin was able to build a career and a life around many different interests. Contrary to traditional advice, he didn't have to choose only one thing. Instead, he chose many things—and for him, this was the work he was born to do.

WHAT SHOULD I DO WITH MY LIFE? (ANSWER: START LIVING)

At my first-ever book signing in New York City many years ago, I watched as people lined up to shake hands and say hi. One of the very first people walked up and asked a question I'll never forget. "Hey," she said, "I don't want to take a lot of your time, so I just have one question. What should I do with my life?"

I laughed and tried to think of some sort of helpful answer, but the bottom line was that I had no idea what to say.

We all face so much pressure over this question. As we've seen throughout this book, most people don't know the best answer right away, and they often change their answer as they go along. But this doesn't mean that there isn't an answer at all. Our goal for this book isn't necessarily to come up with that answer tomorrow; it's to develop the tools to ultimately find that answer, no matter how long it takes. Sometimes finding the work we were born to do may involve refusing to choose a single career path. Even if we can't do *everything*, some of us want to do more than one thing.

Somewhere along the way, most of us were given some terrible advice: you must choose a career niche in order to survive. You must focus on one thing alone to the exclusion of all others, or so you are told, and there is no room for mixing things up or having more than one primary career interest. You can safely place this advice in the paper shredder underneath your desk. There may come a time in your career when you need (and want) to focus on one thing, but until it arrives, you can craft a life around all your interests and still be successful.

A TIME TO X, A TIME TO Y

Let's look back at Devin's story. For a time he had the antiques store. Then he worked in various film production roles. Then he started the travel blog. During some periods his various pursuits overlapped, and during other periods he's pursued a single interest full-time. The point is that life is seasonal. There's a time to explore and experiment, in his journey and in ours, and there's also a time to focus.

Consider the general life cycle that each of us goes through. As we grow up, we make choices, some permanent (we can't go back) and some flexible (we can change our minds later). In big and small ways, our lives change—

we develop relationships, sometimes choose a long-term partner, sometimes have children, and *always* eventually grow old.

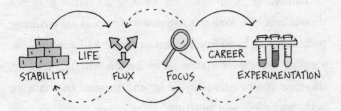

Of course, many life cycles are hardly so smooth. Some of us navigate a bumpy course of many other big changes, both expected and unexpected. We learn to adapt to what happens along the way, but adapting isn't optional. We can't control most of the things that happen to us over the course of our lives, any more than we choose not to grow old.

Just as we have to adapt to the changes throughout our life cycle, so must we adapt to changes throughout our *work cycle.* There may be times in our careers where a stable, traditional 9-to-5 job fits best with where we are in our lives, whether it's because we're raising kids, caring for aging parents, or have other obligations that don't allow us the luxury of draining our savings on a new business idea or venturing out as a "solopreneur." Other times, maybe we're in a place in our lives where we're more willing and able to pursue our entrepreneurial ambitions or experiment with a side hustle or two. Likewise, there are going to be times in our lives when a certain goal or interest takes precedence over all others. In those times, that pursuit—whether it's writing a book or getting into online marketing or joining the circus—will be all we can think about. Finally, there may be times when we'll want to cobble together two or several of these options at once.

Remember, there's no set formula for what a career should look like, and we're all making it up as we go along. Still, jumping from one pursuit or interest to another—or juggling several at a time—can be challenging. Luckily, there's a strategy that can help you navigate that bumpy path. It's called "workshifting."

"WORKSHIFT" YOUR WAY THROUGH LIFE

Though we all try to do it from time to time, it's been scientifically proven that the ability to multitask is largely a myth. Unfortunately, we all have only one brain, and the brain can pay attention only to one task at a time.[*]

Workshifting is different from multitasking—it's where you navigate multiple projects and interests by focusing fully on something for a while, and then deliberately shifting to focus fully on something else. You can do this according to a time-and-calendar method, a project-based method, or simply an intuitive as-you-go method.

---

[*] When you think you're multitasking, you're actually just switching back and forth between tasks, and usually losing a certain amount of energy and processing time during the shift.

Time-Based Workshifting

One day at this, another day at that, or one hour for project A and two for project B—this is how it goes when you use the calendar method to manage multiple responsibilities concurrently.

Elon Musk famously serves as CEO for two major businesses, Tesla Motors and SpaceX. In addition, he regularly announces other big projects and makes worldwide news for completely unrelated ideas. By all accounts, he divides his time by going back and forth between offices, working on one huge set of responsibilities before turning his attention to another.

This may sound intimidating, but you don't have to start a car company and go to space to use a similar workshifting practice. All you need is two or more projects and diligent attention to a scheduling method you devise. Not everyone will work well under these conditions, of course—but some people will thrive.

Outcome-Based Workshifting

I once met someone who owned a busy landscaping business in Alberta, Canada. During the spring and fall, he's busy. During the summer, he's *really* busy. But during the winter, when temperatures regularly drop below freezing and snow is almost always on the ground, the business slows to a halt. Fortunately, the landscaper has another passion. When he's not planting tulip bulbs in anticipation of the first signs of spring, he writes screenplays.

These different interests allow for a seasonal, though atypical, schedule:

> *Summer: all landscaping, all the time*
>
> *Winter: almost all screenplay writing, all the time*
>
> *Spring and fall: a bit of both*

Just as you don't need to be planning to go to space to use time-based workshifting, you don't need to be a landscaper to use outcome-based workshifting. Plenty of people in all sorts of occupations adapt this model in other creative ways. For example, a teacher might build a side hustle in her summers off (after taking a well-deserved vacation). A corporate employee who successfully fights for a sabbatical (see pages 238–241) might write a book while away from the job. There are many ways to make this model work for you, whatever your passions might be.

Instinctive Workshifting

Most of us don't organize our calendars as exactingly as Elon Musk, and we also don't always have seasonal work as tidy as a Canadian landscaper's. What if you just like to do a bunch of stuff, a lot of the time?

If you've been able to create a flexible work environment, like the one that Devin has, you may prefer to plan your activities more instinctively. When considering what to do next, ask yourself, "How does this feel?" and "What would I like to do next?"

Of course, you can also use some combination of these three models. If your work involves commitments to others, as it tends to do for most of us, you'll need to coordinate your meetings and other appointments according to the time-based method at least part of the time. While it's wise to pay attention to how you feel about any given task, you may not *always* be able to do exactly what you want—sometimes there are things that have to be done no matter how you feel. The point about multitasking remains. You shouldn't try to work on a bunch of stuff all the time; you should aim to focus fully on something before deciding to shift to something else.

Last, be aware that workshifting isn't effective for everyone. For some people, it feels helpful and freeing. For others, it feels disruptive. As always, remember the Joy-Money-Flow model and do what works best for *you*.

Q: WHAT SHOULD YOU DO?
A: IT PROBABLY DOESN'T MATTER, SO JUST PICK SOMETHING

There's an old story of a student who approaches his teacher with a problem familiar to many of us. "I have so many ideas!" the student says. "But I don't know which one is best."

"It probably doesn't matter," says the teacher. "Just pick one of them and do it."

The point is that remaining in paralysis is often worse than making any actionable choice. Like it or not, by refusing to make a choice, you've already made a choice to do nothing. And doing something—or several things, even if they turn out to be the wrong thing or things—is almost always better than doing nothing at all. Even when you feel paralyzed and indecisive, you must find a way to take action and move forward.

WORKSHIFTING IN PRACTICE: THE ONLINE COMMUNITY MANAGER

When she graduated from Notre Dame with a dual degree in information technology and English, Kelly Stocker wasn't sure what she'd do with it, but she liked the combination of disciplines. "I figured that we'll probably need computers for a long time," she said, "and I like to read."

She'd grown up in McAllen, Texas, where her father owned a dry cleaning business. At an early age she had a chemistry set and wanted to be a chemist. She built secret clubhouses for her friends, hiding out in the Texas heat, and eventually set her sights on attending the well-respected college in Indiana.

After graduation she traveled in Europe, uploading notes from the trip to early online communities. She booked all her lodging through a site called Hostel World and quickly became loyal to it. When she went from Barcelona to Nice, she wouldn't stay anywhere that wasn't part of the network, and she left user reviews of all her experiences.

Back in the States, job interviews were as uncomfortable for Kelly as they are for most people, especially when they're right out of college. "There's a desperate amount of insecurity when you walk into those situations," she said. "People much older than you are usually sitting on the other side of the desk, making nonverbal judgments about your perceived nature and asking, 'What's your biggest weakness?'"

Still, she landed a job at Dell, back in her home state of Texas but five hours from the small town where she grew up. The job was fine—nothing to write home about, but a good place to grow and gain some valuable experience. Meanwhile, she discovered a whole new world of restaurants and nightlife in Austin, her new hometown. Continuing her passion for writing reviews, she started a newsletter for friends, recommending different places to try.

As you've seen in other stories throughout the book, each of these seemingly random experiences was actually part of an important process. A combination of events— meeting a new friend, receiving a forwarded email, stumbling on the right party—led to Kelly leaving Dell to work for Yelp, the popular online review service. It was a perfect fit for many reasons. First, Kelly had effectively spent years preparing for the job, all without knowing it. Community was her life. She was extroverted and liked to meet people. The degree in information technology was helpful for an Internet company, but her ability to translate concepts between technical and nontechnical people was even more valuable. And then there were those reviews she'd been writing—she knew exactly how the process worked, what made people trust online reviews, and what could be done to encourage a greater experience from all sides.

The responsibilities at the new job were ideal, and so were the working conditions. The work required Kelly to fulfill a variety of roles: a "whack-a-mole" community manager who encouraged new reviewers (while putting down the occasional troll or overly negative complainer), a business development manager who recruited new businesses to advertise, and an event producer several evenings a week.

Completing all these tasks and achieving the high standard to which she held herself required a ton of time—80 hours a week in the beginning, she said—but since there was no office in Austin, Kelly could work at home or wherever she wanted. Her responsibilities were clear, and she could meet them however she saw fit. The unexpected benefit of this arrangement was that the more she did the job, the better she became at it, and it took less time to earn the same salary.

Yelp encourages its community managers to essentially become the "honorary mayor" of the cities they are responsible for. In the first two years of the job, Kelly worked all the time, meeting hundreds of business owners and putting together countless parties and events. All this networking had further benefits. Toward the end of our hour-long conversation, Kelly let it slip that she had "a few other jobs" around the same time. I wondered how that was possible—I'd thought her main job was full-time.

The job at Yelp was indeed full-time, paying a good salary, but after she mastered it she wanted to try other things, too. She became a DJ at a radio station several mornings a week. Using the presentation skills she'd honed by hosting events, she took on a side role at a regional chain of cinemas, hosting interactive sing-alongs. She began writing a column for a local alt-weekly paper. Where did she find the time? She gives an answer common to many people who do what they love: "It's less about how do I find time and more about *why* do I find time. You'll always find time for things that have a strong enough why."

She pursued the side gigs because they met different needs. She really had become an honorary mayor thanks to her tireless efforts throughout the city, and that was good for Yelp. Oh, and all those efforts were good for her, not just her employer.

Kelly loves her job, but she's also built brand equity in herself. She wasn't *only* a great community manager; the sum of the parts was greater than all of the parts on their own.

FLIP THE SCRIPT TO MAKE CHANGE THE DEFAULT CHOICE

Workshifting and juggling multiple projects at the same time can take a lot of self-discipline. By reducing options and making decisions in advance, you'll be better prepared to succeed.

Behavioral economists deploy this method all the time.

One example is an easy hack they use to encourage people to save more for retirement. It all has to do with how a new retirement plan is set up. If the plan is set to automatically withhold funds from your paycheck (known as "opt-out"), you're more likely to agree to a higher savings rate. If you have to take an extra step and actively do something to make sure that money is withheld (known as "opt-in"), the rate plummets.

By applying this kind of thinking to your life and career, you can force yourself to make more positive choices by changing your behavior to opt-out, making the smart or advantageous decision the default choice.

My longtime friend J. D. Roth taught me how to do this using the concepts of "barriers" and "pre-commitment." A *barrier* is something that discourages certain behavior, either positive or negative. For example, J.D. likes to ride his bicycle, but when he moved to a new apartment, he stored the bike in the garage, locked against a rack behind his car, and it was a pain to access. This wasn't an insurmountable problem, but the small annoyance created a barrier to a positive action.

Alternatively, we can use barriers to our advantage. J.D. knows he has a weakness for cookies and ice cream. If sweets are in the house, he'll eat them and won't stop. So when he was getting in better shape (and taking the bike out of the garage more often), he created a "cookie and ice cream barrier" by simply refusing to keep them in the house any longer. Once in a while he'll still buy a cookie, but only when he's out and about, and only one at a time.

A *pre-commitment* is the logical extension of a barrier. With pre-commitment, you create the conditions in advance to lead to your desired behavior or outcome. Want to exercise tomorrow morning? Take out your workout clothes and put them beside your bed tonight. Need to get that work project completed first thing tomorrow? Leave all the files open on your computer, and log out of social media accounts and other time wasters.[*]

THE THREE-TIERED PROJECT BOARD

In 1953, Toyota began using a simplified tracking system to measure progress in the company's car manufacturing and other projects. Most project management systems are highly complex, with hundreds of line items and a large amount of data distributed throughout various timelines.

That's why the *kanban* method, as it came to be called, was shockingly simple. Employees had to be aware of items in only three categories: current, backlog, and completed.

Current: what you're working on now
Backlog: what's coming up
Completed: what you've already finished

If you're a workshifter, you can use this simple technique to keep track of your multiple projects. In some

---

[*] Logging out of social media accounts is a great way to break barriers against procrastination, especially if you're like me and can never remember your passwords.

cases, employees were restricted from working on more than one task at a time, and the *kanban* board provided a visual reminder to keep people on the assigned task. There are even digital *kanban* boards now (the tool is used in software development and other fields), but you can also make one for your office or bedroom using a simple whiteboard. As this image shows, you can simplify the terminology even further:

One tip: don't keep too many things in the "Current" or "Doing" column. The "Backlog" or "To Do" column can contain a number of items, but since you can work on only a few things at once, resist the urge to put more than a few projects or tasks in front of you at once.

Lastly, you may wonder why the "Completed" or "Done" column is needed. Well, I'm not sure what Toyota had in mind long ago, but I love being able to see what I've *finished*, not just what remains. For some reason, it inspires me to keep working on everything else.

THE MULTIPOD LIFE: DIFFERENT WORK MODELS FOR THOSE WHO REFUSE TO CHOOSE

Are you a multipod? As defined by Emilie Wapnick, a young writer and researcher, a multipod, short for "multi-potentialite," is someone who just isn't satisfied with a single career. Emilie's basic principle is that a multipod requires variety. It's not just a nice thing to have; if you're a multipod, you'll be greatly frustrated if you're forced into doing only one thing.

The model of multipotentialism isn't just "do everything you love," because that can also be frustrating. If you're constantly chasing a bunch of different projects, you may never make real progress in any of them. That's why Emilie suggests finding a work model for your multipod life.

Model #1: One Role to Rule Them All

As we've seen throughout the book, some people are able to pursue multiple interests while still organizing them under a single theme. Emilie calls this the "umbrella approach," where tasks and roles may differ but they all tap the same skills and interests. An example might be an architect with a day job who redecorates rental properties on the side, while also teaching design classes one night a week at a local college.

Model #2: Two or More Jobs, with a Clear Division

I once knew a police officer who teaches yoga on Saturdays. She maintains a clear separation between these roles, which don't have a logical overlap and involve totally different skill sets. Every week, she works both jobs (the police one is full-time; the yoga gig is part-time) and doesn't want to give up either one. These jobs stand alone and rarely, if ever, interact.

Model #3: A Job Supports Your Real Interests

Have you heard of Albert Einstein, the famous patent clerk? Probably not—at least not in that way. But working in a boring government office in Switzerland, 40 hours a week, was exactly what he was doing when he developed the theory of relativity. He continued working in the job for several years afterward before finally committing to a full-time university post.

Some people have interests that may not be immediately conducive to making money. In these cases, they may find that it's better to earn their living elsewhere, while reserving enough time and energy to pursue what they *really* love.

For Einstein, the job at the patent office was just fine. Even though it wasn't a thrilling adventure, he could use it to pay his bills and support his real endeavor—you know, that whole relativity thing.

Model #4: To Everything, There Is a Season

This model is for people who are good at going all in with something, but not forever. Maybe it's a part-time job you take just for a summer, or a one-off freelance gig with a set end point. Emilie calls these people "serial careerists" and notes that they usually begin researching their next plan when they're coming to the end of the first one.

Even though people who pursue multiple careers crave variety, having some amount of structure helps to keep you grounded. Choose the model that works best for you.

DOING MORE THAN ONE THING: THE RENAISSANCE MINDSET

Emilie Wapnick, mentioned on page 281, generously agreed to share an exercise she uses with clients who are trying to craft a multifaceted multipod career. Answering these questions shouldn't take long, and they might lead you in a direction you haven't yet considered.

Step 1: Create Your Master List

Make a list of all of your passions and interests, past and present. Star or circle the ones that really pull at your heart right now.

Step 2: Try Out the Common Thread Approach

For each starred item, answer these questions:

- What drew you to this area?
- Do you see any commonalities among your answers?

Then answer these additional questions:

- Which values are most important to you?

- Are there any philosophies that you live by?

- Why do you think you do all of the things you do?

- Can you identify any hidden motivations or driving forces behind your choices?

Step 3: Try Combining Two Unrelated Interests

Is there knowledge related to one area of interest that could be helpful to an audience related to a different interest of yours?

Randomly pair together your list items, filling in the blanks:

_____ for _____.
(interest #1)   (audience related to interest #2)

You may end up with some silly sentences (perhaps "scuba diving for business executives" or maybe "juggling for dogs"), but keep at it. Sometimes the oddest pairings end up being the most lucrative business ideas (though probably not scuba diving for dogs).

I heard of a chef who was so specialized she had narrowed down her field of expertise to raw vegan cooking, specializing in avocados and chia seeds. Some of us are born that way—and sometimes there can be a lot of value in becoming the world's leading expert on [your choice of random topic]. If that's you, and you've decided to lean hard and fast on one specific way of life, good for you. That's great. But for everyone else who's struggling, know that there's another way. You don't *have* to choose a niche. You probably have more than one interest, and that's what makes you interesting.

Pursuing a multifaceted career (or more than one career at once) may require more effort than pursuing a single area of focus. You may find, however, that the reward is well worth the effort. Why not do it all—or at least do a few things well?

You can build a life around all your interests, and you don't have to settle for anything less.

"Finding your dream job doesn't mean it's for life. It's your dream at that particular time and it may change over time as you change. The key is to keep pace with your dreams and that always starts by being attuned to your intuition and the stirrings of your heart."

—SAMANTHA, AGE 40, ENTREPRENEUR AND COACH

13

Winners Give Up
All the Time

OBJECTIVE:

Pursue the Right Opportunities (and Say Farewell to the Wrong Ones)

"Never give up" is bad advice. Real winners won't hesitate to walk away from an unsuccessful venture. Master the art of moving on by learning when to quit and when to keep going.

Have you heard the one about the athlete who faces obstacle after obstacle, refuses to give up, and finally overcomes the odds in the end to win the gold? It makes for a great movie, but in reality most people who aspire to become professional athletes fail. It's simple math, really: for someone to win, many others have to lose. Fortunately, when it comes to finding the work you were born to do, you don't usually have to compete against thousands of other people. And if something isn't working, you don't need to keep going. In fact, you probably shouldn't. Real winners give up all the time.

Lewis Howes was one of those rare athletes who had a real shot at "making it." An All-American in two different sports, he played professional football in an arena league and then made it to the U.S. Olympic team for handball. Unfortunately, fate intervened and shattered both dreams. First he was injured while playing football, and then the handball team failed to advance in a crucial qualifying round.

For most of his early life, Lewis had wanted nothing else other than to be a pro athlete. He'd given his all to the cause, transferring colleges multiple times in search of better playing opportunities, spending his last pennies on protein shakes, and showing off his skills before NFL coaches every chance he got. But now the doors were closing—and no matter how hard he worked, the odds that he'd ever regain the same fitness and ability level he had in his youth were slim.

When Lewis fell, he fell hard. Not having a fallback plan, he ended up sleeping on his sister's couch with his arm in a cast and taking any odd jobs he could get to pay off his mounting credit card debt. This was hardly the life he'd dreamed of while growing up.

But then he realized he could have another dream.

In the space of a few short years, Lewis turned his life

around. He gave up on his ambition to become a professional athlete and began pursuing a different path—a lot of them, actually. He became an entrepreneur and advisor, starting multiple small businesses and helping authors succeed with big book launches. Then he started a podcast, *The School of Greatness*, which encapsulated the lessons of success from CEOs, celebrities, and professional athletes—the same kinds of people Lewis originally aspired to be. The podcast became extremely successful, racking up millions of downloads as Lewis churned out hundreds of episodes.

These days, Lewis says, he feels very lucky. He gave his all to something, and it didn't work out—but instead of becoming bitter and remaining stuck on his sister's couch, he found a way to redirect his energy toward a different series of high-performance goals.

Not everyone in Lewis's situation is as lucky. Many people who "try and try again," only to come short of a big victory, never really recover. Sometimes even the ones who *do* make it struggle later with any kind of meaningful second act. The real secret is that selective quitting is a powerful practice—you just need to learn when to give up and when to keep going.

THE DANGER OF GOING INSANE

You may be familiar with this old adage, often attributed to Albert Einstein: "The definition of insanity is doing the same thing over and over and expecting different results."

Einstein was right in that the real danger of going insane, or just failing over and over, doesn't usually come from doing something new. Rather, the worst failures come from something that we've been doing for a while. Most of us are smart enough to realize that if we try something new and it doesn't work, we can't just keep doing the same thing and expect different results. We might try once more, but we'll usually switch up the tactic. Even mice in a maze will learn to adapt and attempt different solutions if they hit that same dead end enough times.

The greater problem comes when we've become conditioned to success according to a certain method or plan of action. When something works for a while and then it stops working, that's when it's tough to change. We don't keep attempting the same thing over and over because we're stupid, or because we don't know any better. It's just that we love the familiar, and change is hard.

"Why isn't it working?" we ask ourselves. "It worked a thousand times before. Maybe if I just try one more time, that will do it."

Should you get back up and try, try again? Perhaps. But because you're most at risk of repeating failures when you insist on sticking with a method that worked at some point, maybe you should start trying in a very different way.

Let's consider another athlete, one who made it more than a bit further than Lewis Howes. Ever heard of Michael Jordan, the famous baseball player? That's not a typo. For several years, Michael Jordan was one of the most recognized people in the world. He'd achieved his fame by leading the Chicago Bulls to six basketball championships and had broken league records in just about every relevant statistic. Then his 1992 announcement that he would take an early retirement made front-page headlines around the world.

But as famous as he was, what most people didn't know about Michael Jordan was that he also loved baseball, having played as a kid and having continued to follow the sport even as he made his name in a different set of stadiums.

Two years after retiring from basketball, Jordan signed a contract with the Chicago White Sox. He was assigned to a minor league team and dutifully reported to spring training. Not surprisingly, since athletic skills are not usually transferable on a professional level, his talents on the basketball court didn't translate to the baseball field. In fact, it's a wonder he made it as far as he did—he hit several home runs and batted a respectable .252 in one of his two seasons—but this still wasn't far enough. Arguably the best basketball player to have ever lived, Jordan struggled to adapt to the physics of a different sport. So instead of continuing to struggle, he quit.

Jordan returned to basketball, the sport in which he was clearly born to excel, scoring 55 points in a single game within his first two weeks of active play. He went on to win three more back-to-back championships.

WHEN TO GIVE UP AND WHEN TO KEEP GOING

No objective coach would have encouraged Michael Jordan to keep playing baseball, a sport he was only marginally good at. The better path was obvious: he should go back to basketball! When he did, he excelled yet again and continued to dominate the league for many years.

The big decisions you make in your career can have just as much impact on your life as Jordan's decision to return to basketball did for him. Knowing when to give up and when to keep going can feel like an unachievable superpower—but there are three clear strategies you can harness for an advantage.

1. When the Stakes Are Low, Make Changes or Give Up Quickly

Early in the book, I mentioned how I'd changed my college major from accounting to sociology. I made this change fairly quickly, and not entirely by choice: it didn't take long to discover that I simply wasn't good at accounting. If I hadn't quit, I might not have passed my courses. Changing after a semester or two didn't really hold back my education, though. I hadn't taken only accounting classes during those terms; I'd also completed several general education classes that were required for any major, so when I switched to sociology I wasn't far behind in my requirements.

In fact, changing majors probably put me forward, not held me back. If I'd continued to pursue accounting for a

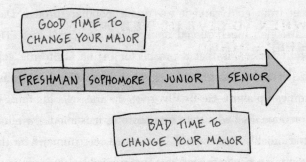

few more semesters before quitting, I would have had a lot more catching up to do, and likely would have struggled to catch up in my new major. Plus, who wants to be the college student who changes his major a dozen times? You don't want to go from department to department and find yourself halfway through college still without a focus. It's much smarter to make changes earlier, when the stakes are low.

> *Changing your major during freshman year = low stakes*
>
> *Changing your major the semester before graduation = higher stakes*

The same kind of analysis applies for decisions of all kinds. Don't waste time on small things, and when the stakes are low, make changes right away.

2. Fight Your FOMO

There's a story that's been told time after time, in sermons and motivational speeches the world over. It's called "three feet from gold," and it was made popular through Dale Carnegie's much-quoted book *Think and Grow Rich*. The short version is that a prospector in the California gold rush tries, tries, and tries again to find riches but always comes up short. He finally gives up and sells his tools to someone else, who then gets more serious about the effort and quickly strikes gold—just three feet from where the original prospector gave up. The implied lesson is obvious: if only the prospector had kept going, he would have found the gold, but he simply gave up too soon.

This is a nice story, but it's also responsible for lots of people remaining stuck in situations that will never pay off. There's no guarantee that the first prospector would have found gold the next day, or even in the next decade. Just as likely, or perhaps even more so, he could have continued to toil in vain. Meanwhile, other doors would be closing and other opportunities drifting away. Just as we don't know what happened with our metaphorical "road not taken," we also don't know what the prospector *gained* by giving up and moving on.

Maybe he took the money he got from selling his tools and made a killing by investing in the cattle farm down the road. Or maybe not—we'll never know. The point is that maybe, just maybe, he ended up a lot better off.

These stories and this kind of thinking are not all Dale Carnegie's fault. The thinking is directly related to the fear of missing out, or FOMO. But while FOMO is a very normal and natural human emotion, it can be dangerous if it prevents you from quitting when it's long past time to give up. After all, if you want to be successful, you can't live your life out of fear.

3. Ignore "Sunk Costs" as Much as Possible

Even if you're not prospecting for gold in the Wild West, chances are that you have to shop for groceries from time to time. Imagine this scenario: it's a busy day at the grocery store, perhaps right after work or before a big holiday, and everyone's stocking up at the store. The cashiers are harried, and there are several carts filled to the brim with bananas, beer, and potato chips in front of you. That's when the moment of decision arrives. You've been dutifully waiting your turn in line, and all of a sudden another lane opens. What do you do? You've already spent 20 minutes waiting in this line . . . maybe you should stick it out.

Meanwhile, the guy behind you, who only spent *two* minutes in line, moves on over. He quickly checks out and goes on his way, while you still have three monster cartfuls to wait for. Your mistake in deciding whether or not to switch lanes (and I've done it many times, too) was to factor the time you've spent waiting into your decision, creating a false commitment to your existing choice even as a more desirable option appeared.

It doesn't matter how much you've invested in something, whether time, money, or any other resource. Next time you're at the grocery store and a better line opens up, take it.

4. Use the Answers to Two Questions to Guide Your Decisions

When the stakes are high and you need to choose whether to give up on any project or course of action, ask yourself these two basic questions:

1. Is it working?
2. Do you still enjoy it?

You don't need to overthink these questions, and you shouldn't sugarcoat the answers. You'll be far more successful in the long term if you're honest with yourself about each of them. Whether it's working or not should be an objective question, and whether you enjoy it or not should be fairly intuitive. If you're not immediately sure about the second question, imagine going a day without thinking about or working on the activity or project. How does that make you feel?

When the answers to both questions are the same, whether yes or no, the decision about whether to give up or keep going should be fairly obvious.

The real challenge comes when the answers are different. When that happens, you have to delve in a bit deeper.

Say you have a business opportunity that makes money, but you don't enjoy doing it. Or presume the opposite—you've been working on something for a while, and you still like it, but it doesn't seem likely to prove successful. You have money but no joy in one of these scenarios, and you have joy but no money in the other.

In this case, you *may* be able to continue being relatively satisfied with the job or project or with the course of action for a period of time, but chances are it's not the thing you were born to do—and you probably won't be totally happy or successful over the long haul. When that happens, it's usually best to start thinking of moving on, even if you stick with it for a while as you plan a transition.

THE FIVE-YEAR MISSION

Daniel Ek, the co-founder and CEO of Spotify, describes himself as a missionary. After selling a previous business for a lot of money, he initially "retired" to a life of partying. When he discovered that fast cars and expensive champagne provided only a temporary form of happiness, he gave up on retirement and started one of the world's largest music streaming services.

But to avoid burning out as he had in his first job, Ek came up with a clever strategy—he gave himself a five-year "expiration date." "Five years is long enough for me to achieve something meaningful, but short enough so I can change my mind every few years," Ek told the *New Yorker*. "I'm on my second five-year commitment on Spotify. In two years, I will have to make my next one. I will need to ask myself if I still enjoy what I'm doing. I'm kind of unusual that way, but it gives me clarity and purpose."

Ek's cycle of five-year missions is a classic example of serially resetting, albeit with a specific end date that is decided on in advance. True, the timeline restricts options but also provides *urgency*. If you knew you had only two years to complete a mission before forcing yourself to quit, how would you change your approach?

LIFE DETOX: MAKE A LIST OF THINGS TO GIVE UP

We all have bad habits we'd like to quit. Whether it's caffeine, sugar, trashy TV shows, or something else, if you've ever tried to give up something, you know that's not usually that easy. All of a sudden you have cravings for red velvet cupcakes and an extra-large peppermint mocha, even if you never cared for them before.

There's another kind of detox that's much easier, though. If you work with other people in any capacity, you may occasionally fall into bad habits that sap your productivity—behaviors that accomplish little while taking your limited time away from more important things. When giving up these bad habits, you'll see immediate benefits and almost no downsides or weird cravings. Here are a few good ones to try.

GIVE UP THE NEED FOR PETTY CONTROL OF USELESS THINGS.

You don't need to be copied on every email or informed of every decision. If the right things are happening, don't interrupt the flow. And even if they aren't, do you really need to triage an extra 200 messages every day?

GIVE UP THE DESIRE TO BUILD YOUR IMAGE WITHOUT DOING ANYTHING SUBSTANTIAL.

Looking good in the eyes of colleagues is a worthy goal, but you'll look the best when you make real progress on shared goals. Before sending an email or taking on a task or project that may be unnecessary, ask yourself, "Does this matter?"

GIVE UP THE IMPOSSIBLE DREAM OF STAYING ON TOP OF EVERYTHING.

If you try to do everything, inevitably you'll fall behind. Understand your role, whether as part of an organization or as part of humanity in general, and take ownership of the areas of responsibility entrusted to you. Don't worry about the other stuff; if you're doing your job well, you probably won't be able to keep up with it anyway, and that's okay.

These are just a few ideas of bad work habits to give up. Make your own list and give up something today.

CREATE SECURITY SO THAT YOU *CAN* GIVE UP (WITHOUT GOING BROKE)

An emergency savings account provides security in the event of lost assets, whether due to a lost job, a natural disaster, or just a broken washing machine. But as I've explained elsewhere, your relationships are always your greatest assets. So why do so few of us have an emergency savings account for our relationships?

The social network LinkedIn is an interesting model for thinking about this. If you've ever made a LinkedIn profile, you've probably added various details about your education, employment, and skills. Then you've gone on to make "connections" with people you know, usually based on your email address book or company directory. (Remember: in any social network, avoid the temptation to think of people so abstractly; they aren't just fans or "followers.")

If you use LinkedIn or any similar service over time, each time you log in you'll be accumulating updates from your connections, and you may begin receiving more and more invitations of your own to connect with others. It's essentially a relationship hub, in the same way a to-do list is a hub to keep track of tasks or a calendar is a hub to keep up with appointments.

You can use this hub (or any other, if LinkedIn isn't your thing) to create a "relationship savings account" that will help you feel more comfortable with making a big transition or giving something up because you'll be more secure in the knowledge that you've got people who are available to help during a period of uncertainty. It's not about amassing the world's greatest collection of business cards; it's about building genuine relationships to keep in the bank for a rainy day. And don't wait for that rainy day to start adding to your relationship savings account, because by then it will be too late. Instead, start right away.

Here are some actions to take now:

- Add any new people you've met recently as contacts to your main social networking accounts

- Ask co-workers what they're working on and if you can do anything to help them

- Be proactive by reaching out to offer your contacts something specific, whether it's letting someone in on a job opening or opportunity, introducing them to someone else in your network, or even sending them a copy of a book you found interesting

- Practice a random act of kindness

Just as regular deposits in your savings account or retirement plan will grow over time, so too will regular investments in your relationship bank accounts.

IF YOU MISS 100 PERCENT OF THE SHOTS, GET OFF THE ICE

Every success book has a chapter on how different famous people overcame the odds and never gave up, eventually achieving their dreams. You've heard these stories many times: the world-class author who was rejected by a hundred publishers before finally being accepted and eventually winning the Nobel Prize in literature, the inventor whose first thousand inventions flopped before he hit it big with some game-changing innovation, and on and on.

"You miss 100 percent of the shots you don't take," a motivational quote attributed to hockey legend Wayne Gretzky, is often deployed to reinforce these stories. It's true in its literal sense: sure, if you don't take the shot, you won't make it. But if you keep missing the net over and over, maybe you shouldn't take the same kind of shot. And in real life, just as in a real hockey game, the reality is that you don't get a chance to keep trying and trying indefinitely. The coach will pull you from the starting lineup. Your teammates will stop passing you the puck. They'll make up another saying: "We miss 100 percent of the shots that we pass to that guy"—and the opportunities to score will stop coming your way.

Contrary to popular belief, if you want to win, you shouldn't always just keep going. You should regroup and try something totally different. "Winners never quit, and quitters never win" is a lie. To win, sometimes you need to find a new game to play.

Appendix 1: Tool Kit

Throughout the book, we examined a number of principles and strategies. Here's a summary of many of them. You can also find many more tools and resources at BornforThisBook.com.

1. *There's more than one possible path. Use the Joy-Money-Flow model to find the best one.*

There are plenty of things you *could* do with your career, but the people who are most successful have found the perfect combination of joy, money, and flow. They've won the career lottery—and they don't have to choose between their money and their life. Above all else, finding the work you were meant to do should be your number one career goal.

2. *Craft backup plans. They will allow you to take more risks and make better choices.*

There's no shame in having a plan B, or even plans C–Z. Use the "if this, then that" method to make a backup plan for every career choice, and then make a backup for the backup. If one strategy doesn't work, move to the next.

3. *Make a commitment to resign your job every year.*

Once a year, on the date of your choosing, commit to yourself that you will quit your job *unless staying put is the best possible choice for you at this time.* If it is, that's great—you can proceed with confidence, knowing that you're on the right track. If not, immediately begin looking for something different.

4. Improving "soft skills" can increase your value no matter what kind of career you have.

Hard skills are things you learned through technical or academic training: how to make architectural drawings with certain software, how to properly administer medication as a nurse, and so on. Soft skills are just as important—if not more—but aren't usually taught in school. To be more effective (and to become more valuable), spend time improving your soft skills in writing, negotiation, conflict management, and follow-up.

5. Stop storing things in your head.

Your head is not a good library. Always write down your tasks, next steps, and ideas. If you're looking for a good business idea, write down everything you know about a specific topic that other people ask you about. Go step by step and share everything that makes it easy for you. Then, once it's out of your head, see what you can make of it.

6. Choose your own job title.

Select the title you want, not an existing one. Write a job description of your future expertise and responsibilities. Determine what it will take to achieve that role; then work backwards from the goal.

7. Hack your job to create the best possible working conditions.

If you work for a company or organization, build security by becoming indispensable and seeking to improve the company's bottom line. When the time is right, consider taking an in-house or out-of-house sabbatical to regroup and improve your skills further.

8. Create a "side hustle" even if you never plan to work on your own full-time.

Side projects provide security, and no one should have all his or her income coming from only one source. Use the 19 Days to Hustle plan (see page 161) to create an all-new source of income. If you know what you're doing, use the 24-Hour Product challenge (see page 167) to finish even quicker.

9. *Don't fear commitment.*

It's okay to make mistakes—and change course to correct them—but eventually you should choose something. You shouldn't worry about making a single mistake, or even a lot of them. Everyone makes mistakes, and what matters is how you recover. Eventually, though, you want your mistakes to bring you closer to the work you were meant to do. And the closer you get, the more selective you should be.

10. *If something isn't working, give up.*

Sure, you miss all the shots you don't take, but maybe you shouldn't take some of those shots in the first place. And if you miss shot after shot, eventually you'll get benched, and you won't have the same opportunities. Don't just try, try again, in other words—try something different. "Winners never quit" is another misguided assumption. Real winners quit all the time . . . sometimes right before they go on to win the lottery.

Appendix 2: "Here's How I'll Make You a Lot of Money" (Email Pitch)

In Chapter 3, I told the story of Vanessa Van Edwards sending a cold pitch to Creative Live, an online educational company. Vanessa could have gone through a referral, but she chose an approach that initially seemed risky: writing to the general support email address on the website.

I thought you'd enjoy seeing how she set up the big proposal. Can you do something like this in your own way?

The message below is exactly what she sent.

> *Subject: Here's How I Plan to Make Creative Live a Lot of Money*
>
> Dear Creative Live Team,
>
> I am a huge fan of your platform and want to help you create your next awesome course. I am a behavioral investigator and author specializing in human lie detection and body language.
>
> I write for the *Huffington Post* and teach courses and seminars on body language online and to live audiences around the world.
>
> I would love to do a course on human lie detection and body language for Creative Live. I have made

over $20,000 in course sales on Udemy only in the
first three months without any promotion. This is a
topic people love, and I love to teach it.

I think Creative Live would be an amazing platform for this course. Please let me know if you would
be open to having me pitch your team on the topic.
I am happy to jump through hoops, perform magic,
and move mountains to teach on Creative Live.

I have attached a proposal for your review.

Best,
Vanessa
P.S. In my proposal I have testimonials, course reviews, and a slide called "Why This Course Will Sell"
on my planned marketing strategy for you.

Was it worth it? Here's a final note from Vanessa: "Teaching
at Creative Live ended up being one of the best moments of my
life. I remember waking up on day 3 of filming and thinking I
had the best job in the world. It was totally worth the pitch!"

Appendix 3: Never Lose at Tic-Tac-Toe (Bonus Lesson!)

I hope this book has taught you a number of helpful lessons. If not, at least you can learn to play tic-tac-toe better. Armed with this info, you will never again lose—you can only win or tie. Here's all you need to know:

1. If you go first, always start with the center piece or one of the four corner pieces. Never play the middle-of-the-edge piece unless defending against a near-win.

2. If your opponent goes first, always respond with the center piece (as long as your opponent didn't choose it) or a corner piece. In no circumstance should you choose a middle-of-the-edge piece in the first round of the game.

3. Whether you or your opponent began the game, if he or she makes any sort of mistake, you should be able to convert the game into a win. If he or she plays well, you'll tie. But no matter what, as long as you stay away from the edges in the beginning of the game, and only play an edge to defend or win later, you'll never lose.

Oh, and if you'd like to get more tactical, check out this optimal strategy guide.

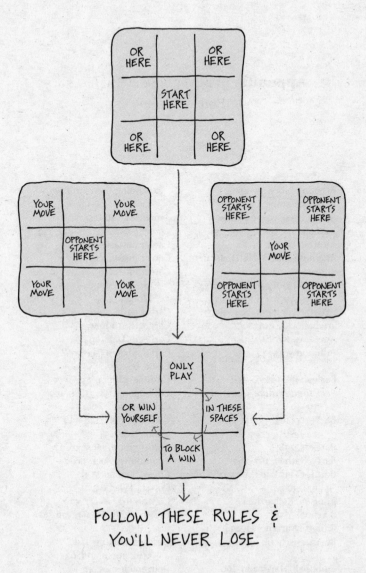

FOLLOW THESE RULES &
YOU'LL NEVER LOSE

Index

Do what you love and work better to live more
Find the quest that will bring purpose to your life

Entrepreneur, blogger, founder of the World Domination Summit, life hacker extraordinaire, and *New York Times* bestselling author Chris Guillebeau shares a manifesto on adventure, self-employment, and giving back in *The $100 Startup*, and teaches readers about finding meaning by committing to a life-changing quest in *The Happiness of Pursuit*.